The Pleasures of English Food

THE
PLEASURES
OF
ENGLISH
FOOD

*Alan
Davidson*

English 🐧 Journeys

PENGUIN BOOKS

Published by the Penguin Group
Penguin Books Ltd, 80 Strand, London WC2R 0RL, England
Penguin Group (USA) Inc., 375 Hudson Street, New York, New York 10014, USA
Penguin Group (Canada), 90 Eglinton Avenue East, Suite 700, Toronto, Ontario, Canada M4P 2Y3
(a division of Pearson Penguin Canada Inc.)
Penguin Ireland, 25 St Stephen's Green, Dublin 2, Ireland
(a division of Penguin Books Ltd)
Penguin Group (Australia), 250 Camberwell Road, Camberwell, Victoria 3124, Australia
(a division of Pearson Australia Group Pty Ltd)
Penguin Books India Pvt Ltd, 11 Community Centre, Panchsheel Park, New Delhi – 110 017, India
Penguin Group (NZ), 67 Apollo Drive, Rosedale, North Shore 0632, New Zealand
(a division of Pearson New Zealand Ltd)
Penguin Books (South Africa) (Pty) Ltd, 24 Sturdee Avenue, Rosebank, Johannesburg 2196, South Africa

Penguin Books Ltd, Registered Offices: 80 Strand, London WC2R 0RL, England

www.penguin.com

These extracts taken from *The Penguin Companion to Food*, first published 2002
Published in Penguin Books 2009
1

Copyright © Alan Davidson, 2002
All rights reserved

Set by Rowland Phototypesetting Ltd, Bury St Edmunds, Suffolk
Printed in England by Clays Ltd, St Ives plc

Except in the United States of America, this book is sold subject
to the condition that it shall not, by way of trade or otherwise, be lent,
re-sold, hired out, or otherwise circulated without the publisher's
prior consent in any form of binding or cover other than that in
which it is published and without a similar condition including this
condition being imposed on the subsequent purchaser

ISBN: 978-0-141-19102-7

www.greenpenguin.co.uk

Mixed Sources
Product group from well-managed
forests and other controlled sources
www.fsc.org Cert no. SA-COC-1592
© 1996 Forest Stewardship Council

Penguin Books is committed to a sustainable future
for our business, our readers and our planet.
The book in your hands is made from paper
certified by the Forest Stewardship Council.

Afternoon tea: one of a pair of tea meals (the other being high tea), both of which are essentially British and which, although alike in having tea as the beverage served, stand in high contrast to each other in other respects.

Mrs Beeton expressed succinctly the material difference when she remarked that 'There is Tea and Tea' and went on to say that 'A "High Tea" is where meat takes a more prominent part and signifies really, what is a tea-dinner ... The afternoon tea signifies little more than tea and bread-and-butter, and a few elegant trifles in the way of cake and fruit.'

Although the custom of taking a cup of tea, at least occasionally, at a suitable time in the afternoon may have been adopted by some ladies in the late 17th century, it seems clear that neither afternoon tea nor high tea, the meals, started to become established until late in the 18th or early in the 19th centuries. Since almost all authors rely on the indefatigable Ukers, who had scoured available literary and artistic sources for indications on this point, he must be allowed here to speak for himself:

Dr Alexander Carlyle wrote in his autobiography of the fashionable mode of living at Harrowgate in 1763 that, 'The ladies gave afternoon tea and coffee in their turn.' For the custom of afternoon tea as a distinct and definite function, however, the world is indebted to Anna, wife of the seventh Duke of Bedford, 1788–1801. In her day, people ate prodigious breakfasts. Luncheon was a sort of picnic, with no servants in attendance. There was no other meal until eight o'clock dinner, after which tea was served in the drawing-room. The Duchess of Bedford struck out a new line; she had tea and cakes served at five o'clock, because, to quote herself, she had 'a sinking feeling'.

Fanny Kemble, the actress, in her *Later Life*, records that she first became acquainted with afternoon tea in 1842 at Belvoir Castle, seat of the Dukes of Rutland. She added that she did not believe the now universally-honored custom dated back any further than this.

In the 20th century afternoon tea has kept to a formula: tea (in a pot, with milk and sugar, or perhaps lemon if China tea is served); dainty small sandwiches (cucumber, very thinly sliced, is a favoured filling); scones with butter and jam (optional); some form of little cakes or slices of a large cake; biscuits (optional); and a serviette or napkin to complete the generally dainty picture. The effect is charming and may be achieved by a hostess (or host) with far less expenditure of effort and money than a full meal, or even a high tea, would require.

A variant of afternoon tea is the Devon cream tea, which towards the end of the 20th century was advancing relentlessly across all the other counties of England, and indeed appearing in Scotland, Wales and Ireland, sometimes described as just 'cream tea'. This calls for scones, clotted cream, and jam.

Apples: In Britain apples are divided clearly into eating and cooking varieties, a distinction which is much less rigid in other countries. (An English cooking apple disintegrates to a purée when cooked. This effect is brought about by a high content of malic acid, which is characteristic of early, soft, green-skinned apples of the Codlin type, such as Grenadier; and of the late, long-keeping, red-striped Lane's Prince Albert family which includes the familiar Bramleys.)

As for eating apples, the British are catholic in their taste. It may still be possible to discern some traces of the effects produced by the Victorian and Edwardian custom of taking dessert with port; this prompted enthusiasm for apples with a 'nutty' flavour which would complement the port. It was also partly responsible for a small tide of gastronomic prose about apples which washed over England in the late 19th and early 20th centuries and which embodied language which resembled writing about fine wines. But none of this had much effect on the vast majority of British people. They accept with docile pleasure the imported Golden and Red Delicious, but their greatest favourite is still the Cox. They are not deterred by the curious appearance of the Russets, which has caused these to be neglected in other countries.

STORAGE AND PRESERVATION, AND
APPLE PRODUCTS

Storing apples is simple in principle, but exacting in practice. The requirements are that the apples should be of a well-keeping – which means late – variety; that they should be absolutely sound, for even a small bruise or a break in the skin releases enzymes which hasten decay; that the place should be dry and cool; and that the apples should not touch each other, lest infection be spread by contagion.

The practical details were understood early. Pliny the Elder (Ist century AD) warned against trying to store windfalls or apples picked on wet days. He recommended a cool, dry room with windows on the side away from the sun which could be opened on warm days. The apples were to be stored in a way that would permit free circulation of air around them.

From early times apples were preserved by drying. The usual method in medieval Europe was to peel and core the apples and dry them whole, threaded on strings: this required a warm and airy drying room. The later method of cutting apples across into rings is more reliable, since these dry faster.

An unusual old drying method was the preparation of Norfolk 'biffins'. These were apples which were dried, whole and unpeeled, in warm bread ovens so that they shrivelled into a form like roundish, red prunes. The partial cooking helped to preserve them. They were close packed in layers as they dried. The *pommes tapées* of the Loire Valley in France are somewhat similar, but are peeled first; then dried in special ovens for about five days, during which they are occasionally 'tapped' with a mallet to encourage them to subside into a flattish shape, for ease of storage. It is usual to soak them in red wine before eating them. Similar treatment produced *poires tapées* in the past but, although they were famous in the 19th century, these have virtually disappeared.

APPLE VARIETIES

Allington Pippin is one of the sweet/sharp varieties which exemplifies the manner in which an apple's taste can change with age. As Joan Morgan points out, it 'can be almost bitter sweet in early November but mellows to a definite pineapple flavour by Christmas'. It also exemplifies complexity of flavour; one enthusiast claimed that he had found 'pine and grape, the scent of quince and pear . . . the breath of honey from the hive in its gelid pores'.

Bismarck, unusual among British-type cooking apples in having a bright red skin, was introduced from Tasmania, its place of origin, in 1890.

Blenheim Orange, one of the best apples of the Pippin family, was popular in England for a century after its introduction around 1818. It is large, dull yellow and red, and has crisp flesh and a flavour of unusually acid quality. Season: midwinter, so traditionally a Christmas apple.

Bramley's Seedling or Bramley, the most widely sold cooking apple in Britain, has a very long keeping season, from early autumn right through to next summer. It is usually very large and often irregular in shape. It is harvested commercially as a green apple, or green with faint red stripes, but will turn yellow if left on the tree; and there are also crimson varieties.

Costard, an extinct family of British apples, was one of the first types to have a distinct name, which was already in use in the 13th century. The first important kitchen apple, large and flavourful, much used in pies until it began to disappear towards the end of the 17th century. 'Costard' was medieval slang for 'head'. The name survives in the word 'costermonger', although such a person may now sell any kind of fruit or vegetable.

Cox's Orange Pippin, one of the best of the large family of Pippins. Since its introduction in the first half of the 19th century it has become the most popular British apple. It is a medium-sized, round apple, dull brownish-green with faint red stripes and a red flush on one side. It usually has a matt brown russeted area around the stem. The texture is crisp, the flavour solidly acid but balanced by sweetness. The skin is strongly scented and should be eaten. Season: late autumn to spring, but the best is midwinter.

Delicious, a red apple, whose name is often applied by an inept abbreviation to the unrelated Golden Delicious. Delicious began as a chance seedling on the farm of Jess Hiatt of Peru, Iowa, in 1872. He marketed it as Hiatt's Hawkeye. Stark Brothers, a large fruit-growing concern, bought out Hiatt and renamed the variety Delicious. Since the 1940s it has been the leading American apple, is also widely grown elsewhere and has given rise to new varieties such as Starking (sometimes Star King). The fruit is large, red, and elongated, with five projections at the bottom end. The flavour is sweet but insipid, lacking in acid. Season: autumn to early winter.

Ellison's Orange is highly flavoured, tasting of aniseed and pear drops.

Flower of Kent, a large, green variety now almost forgotten, but said to be the apple whose fall inspired Sir Isaac Newton to formulate his law of universal gravitation.

Gillyflower, a variety mentioned by many early authors such as Evelyn (1699) and praised for its rich and aromatic flavour.

Gladstone, a large early summer apple of pleasing flavour and aroma.

Granny Smith is unusual, perhaps unique, in being a brilliant, almost emerald, green even when fully ripe. Much grown in warm climates, notably in S. Africa, Australia, Chile, and France. The texture is crisp and juicy, the flavour distinctive, with a hint of almond.

James Grieve, an English apple classified as 'early dessert', has a pleasantly balanced flavour and yields plenty of delicious juice.

Laxton apples, a large and important group, owe their name to the horticulturist Thomas Laxton (1830–90), whose sons produced thousands of cross-bred apples, from which many of the best British dessert apples are derived. A high proportion of them retain the family name Laxton. They bear a general resemblance to Coxes, but are usually brighter green, with less striping and russeting. The texture is crisp and the flavour light. The best-known late Laxtons include Laxton's Pearmain and

Laxton's Superb. Laxton's Fortune is a yellow and red striped mid-season variety.

Pearmain, the oldest English apple name, was recorded in a Norfolk document of 1204. It is derived from the old French apple name 'parmain' or 'permain', referring perhaps to a group of apples rather than a single variety. All that modern Pearmains have in common is the green and red colouring typical of many British apples. The best known is Worcester Pearmain, an early autumn apple which has a good, sharp flavour, with a hint of strawberry, and a crisp texture when fresh, but does not keep. Its red parts are distinctively dark. Most other Pearmains ripen later.

Pippin, originally meaning any apple grown from a pip, is a name derived from the French 'pépin', meaning both 'pip' and the apple. By the 16th century the term had come to denote a hard, late-ripening, long-keeping apple of acid flavour. The first pippins brought over from France to England were cider apples, but eating varieties were soon developed. In relatively recent times Ribston Pippin became popular, and from it Cox's Orange Pippin was bred. Sturmer Pippin does well in the southern hemisphere, notably S. Africa and Australia.

In America the name 'Pippin' was used for different kinds of apple, the most famous being a purely American variety, Newtown Pippin.

Russet is the name of a group of apples with distinctive matt brown skin, often spotted or with a faint red flush, and of a flattened lopsided shape. The flesh is crisp and the apples keep well. The flavour is unusual and pearlike.

Russets are used both for eating and for cooking. Their

size varies from tiny to very large. Royal Russet, a variety known in England before the 17th century, remains popular on the mainland of Europe as a cooking apple. In Britain Egremont Russet and Golden Russet are the most popular kinds. An American variety, Roxbury Russet, is claimed to have originated in Roxbury, Massachusetts, in the early 17th century. If true, this would make it America's oldest named variety.

White Joaneting, an English apple known before 1600 (the Jenneting of Elizabethan writers), is still sometimes grown because it ripens before any other apple, in July. Its shiny skin is yellow, sometimes with a red flush. It has a good flavour and is juicy, but does not keep.

Worcester apples form a group of which the Worcester Pearmain is the best known. Firm, sweet flesh with a strawberry flavour is characteristic of them.

APPLES IN COOKERY

Before the introduction of the domestic oven apples were roasted whole in front of an open fire. Practical difficulties in cooking them evenly led to the development of more complicated 'apple roasters'. These were metal racks incorporating curved tinplate reflectors to heat the far side of the apples.

Apple pie is perhaps the most famous apple dish, and exhibits interesting variations. The American apple pie, with pastry underneath and on top, is derived from the medieval raised pies (of which the British pork pie and French *pâté en croute* are surviving examples) and various sweet and savoury dishes completely enclosed in 'coffyns' or pastry cases. In contrast, the modern British apple pie is normally baked in a deep pie dish with a crust on top only. This form too has a long history, since pies with an upper crust only had emerged as early as the 17th century. It was common in Britain to add verjuice for extra sharpness; and old recipes often included quinces which not only sharpened the flavour but gave an attractive pink colour.

The standard accompaniment for apple pie is cream. A recipe of 1704, written in heroic couplets by the little-known poet Leonard Welsted (not, as sometimes stated, the work of satirist William King) cautions against tasting the pie until the cream has had an opportunity to 'give a softness to the tarter juice'. (The recipe sounds good. It includes quinces, brown sugar, cloves, and a little orange flower water.) It is a modern American practice to serve the pie with ice cream, giving an attractive contrast of heat and cold. In Britain it was often eaten with cheese, especially Derby.

Apple cakes are made by several different methods. In England they are plain cakes based on creamed or rubbed-in mixtures with chopped or grated raw apples, and are a speciality of the southwest.

Bacon: the side of a pig cured with salt in a single piece. The word originally meant pork of any type, fresh or cured, but this older usage had died out by the 17th century.

Bacon, in the modern sense, is peculiarly a product of the British Isles, or is produced abroad to British methods, specifically for the British market. Denmark is the leader in this field. In Britain itself, many regional variations on cuts and cures for bacon exist. It was formerly sold by cheesemongers, rather than butchers, and the association is still maintained in some shops.

Preserved pork, including sides salted to make bacon, held a place of primary importance in the British diet in past centuries. Pigs were kept by everyone, fed economically on scraps, waste, and wild food. Their salted and smoked meat was useful to give savour to otherwise stodgy dishes, and was especially important for the poor. Cobbett, in *Cottage Economy* (1823), considered the possession of a couple of flitches of bacon did more for domestic harmony than 'fifty thousand Methodist sermons and religious tracts. The sight of them upon the rack tends more to keep a man from stealing than whole volumes of penal statutes.' Victorian and early 20th-century investigations into the conditions of the poor discovered that bacon was a staple of all households except for the most poverty stricken. At this time, it was thought desirable that bacon should be very fat; bacon fat and lard were then much more important sources of fat in the British diet than they now are.

British pigs for both fresh and salted meat had been much improved in the 18th century. During the 19th, Yorkshire Large Whites, Middle Whites, Tamworths, and Lincolnshire curly-coated pigs were the breeds favoured for bacon. However, in mid-century the Danes, seeking a new market for their pigs, bred a very productive bacon pig, the Landrace, and began to export large amounts of bacon to Britain. Nowadays many bacon pigs are hybrids, with Yorkshire Large White and Landrace prominent in their make-up.

The first large-scale bacon curing business was set up in the 1770s by John Harris in Wiltshire. (The Harris firm still exists, though it was taken over by a larger corporation in 1962.) Until this time pigs for London's bacon had been driven long distances on foot before being killed there, which exhausted them and spoiled the meat. Harris realized that it would be more practical to make the bacon where the pigs were and send that to London.

Wiltshire remains the main bacon-producing area of Britain, and the standard commercial method of curing bacon is known as the 'Wiltshire cure'. This was originally a dry cure. The prepared sides of the pig (legs still on, for this method) were strewn with salt and stacked skin side down. (It is during this process that a chemical change, aided by salt-tolerant bacteria and the presence of small amounts of nitrate in the 'pickle', produces the characteristic pink colour of the lean.) After 10 to 14 days, the salt was brushed off and the sides matured for a week before packing. Since the First World War, however, brine has been used, both injected into the sides, and for soaking, in place of dry salt. After maturing, the sides may be smoked.

A Wiltshire side is a large piece of meat, and is divided up for various purposes. The shoulder yields the cheapest bacon; the most valued is back and streaky bacon (from the loin region and the belly respectively); while the legs, removed after curing, provide what is called gammon; and other parts of the side may become 'boiling bacon'.

The Wiltshire cure is but one of a number of techniques, reflecting regional preferences for bacon types; while people in the south of England favoured Wiltshire bacon smoked over oak or pine sawdust, people in the north liked 'green bacon' (unsmoked and often cured separately from the legs). Ayrshire bacon, a supremely good Scottish version, is made from skinned and boned meat, rolled and lightly cured. The dry method of curing bacon is still used on some farms; bacon so made is distinguished by its dryness and firmness.

The main British use of bacon is in the thin slices called rashers (formerly, collops), often fried and served with eggs. Although associated with the 'traditional' English breakfast, this combination is a favourite meal at more or less any time of day. Larger pieces of bacon, or bacon hocks, boiled and served hot or cold with mustard, were much used as standby dishes in poorer households. There are, or were, all kinds of economical dishes, intended to make a little bacon go a long way: cereal and pulse pottages were early items in this group. Somewhat later, bacon pudding was a common dish in many parts of Britain, in times when every cottager kept a pig. Most regional varieties are suet rolls, or sometimes round puddings, containing bacon, onion, and often sage.

Banbury cakes: are named after the town in Oxfordshire with which they have been associated since at least the 17th century. The cakes were sold from a shop there in 1638, by one Betty White according to some local records. (This shop, in Parsons Street, was certainly known as 'The Original Banbury Cake Shop' in 1833 and its history is documented since then, including the export in the 19th century of considerable numbers of the cakes to India.)

The first known recipe, by Gervase Markham (1615), required a rich, sweet, spiced, yeast-leavened dough to be divided into two portions. One was left plain, and the other was mixed with currants. The portion with the currants in was then sandwiched between thin layers of plain paste. If the quantities given in the recipe were used to make just one cake, the final product would have been very large, weighing about 4 kg (8 lb). Similar cakes were known elsewhere, one example being the Shrewsbury simnel cake; in Scotland, one has survived down to the present day in the form of black bun, made at New Year.

By the first part of the 19th century, recipes show that Banbury cakes could be made either as large flat pastries, scored and broken into oblong pieces after baking, or as individual confections enclosed in puff pastry, similar to those still known.

Dorothy Hartley says that the cakes 'used to be carried around, all hot and crisp and fresh, in specially made chip baskets, wrapped in white cloths'. She adds that they were always eaten fresh and hot.

Modern Banbury cakes are small and oval, made of light flaky pastry with a crisp top achieved by a powdering of sugar before baking. The filling is of butter, chopped peel, dried fruit, sugar, and mixed spice.

Eccles cakes are similar to Banbury cakes.

Banquet: the English word, and its close relations in other languages (French *banquet*, Italian *banchetto*, etc.) have had different meanings at different times. Today, the meaning of banquet in English is: a formal and sumptuous meal, usually of a ceremonial nature and for a large number of people. The word embraces the meal in its entirety.

However, in the 16th and 17th centuries this was not so. The whole of a formal and sumptuous meal would then have been called a feast; and the word 'banquet', at that time, referred to the final, sweet, course or episode of the feast. This often took place in a separate room, not the one in which the main part of the feast had been consumed; and its character was different.

In medieval times, it had been common for wine and spices to be served as the finale to any important meal, after the tables had been cleared. The purpose of this ceremony, called the 'voidée' in accordance with its French origin, was originally medicinal. The spices and the spiced wine were selected and prepared in a manner thought to aid digestion.

However, the serving of these items sometimes became merged with the serving of the last course of the feast, which consisted in various sweetmeats and which was also modelled on a French practice. And as time passed, the two things were separated again, but now in reverse sequence; the spiced wine was served first, and this was followed by the service of sweetmeats.

Hence the interesting and pleasant characteristics of the English banquet of those times. Some nobles began to design and build special rooms, or even special buildings, for their banquets. These were often secluded; not necessarily by being built some way from the main house – there was a fashion for building them on the roof. One can imagine the merriment with which the important guests would file along a corridor and then mount perhaps several staircases, finally emerging from a small circular staircase onto the roof, enjoying a panorama of the surrounding countryside, and passing into a small private room in which the sweetmeats would be laid out ready, with exquisite artistry.

Often, there would be no servants; or, if there was one, he would be gone once he had seen to it that the guests were all present and comfortable. Part of the pleasure lay in the 'withdrawn' and private atmosphere of the banquet, when people could relax completely, indulge in indiscreet talk, and so forth.

The scent of flowers and the sound of music, being played by musicians who were nearby but out of sight, could complete the charming environment.

Examples of banqueting rooms given by Jennifer Stead include the earliest known banqueting room on a roof, that of Sir William Sharington, who, in the middle of the 16th century, had an octagonal lookout tower incorporating two banqueting rooms, which still survive.

A banqueting room could also be set in a garden; in the Renaissance period the garden itself was seen as a source of inspiration and refreshment for intellect and spirit and senses alike, one might say a banquet for the mind as well as a feast for the eyes. Indeed, the room might itself be made of garden materials. Queen Elizabeth caused a temporary banqueting house to be erected in Greenwich Park for the entertainment of the French Ambassador and his staff. This was made entirely of boughs and blossoms. And at Cobham Hall in Kent a living lime tree was converted into a banqueting house comprising three rooms at different levels, with stairs between them, and accommodating fifty people in all.

The theme of water was generally popular, and the sound of water splashing in a fountain was considered to be a highly appropriate background noise for banquets. It was not uncommon to combine the function of 'water house' (a building which housed the pumps and pipes which supplied water to the house and to the gardens) with that of banqueting room. And some banqueting rooms took the form of grottoes, where elaborate decorations of sea shells and a damp atmosphere conducive to the growth of ferns and suchlike plants created a wettish environment which was thought to have particular charm.

All this has long been lost. Few are the instances in modern times of a 'banquet' which offers true pleasure to the participants.

Batter: is a semi-liquid preparation consisting of eggs, milk, and flour in varying proportions. Lighter batters can be made by replacing some of the milk with water or beer.

One of the main uses of batter is to coat foods which are to be deep fried, either little pieces of vegetable, fish, meat, fruit to make fritters or larger items, such as fish fillets. The texture and viscosity of the mixture is important, for it must be thick enough to adhere to the food, but not so thick that the coating becomes excessive and heavy. The batter cooks very quickly in the hot fat and forms a crisp shell around the food, preventing scorching, whilst retaining flavour and juices.

Wherever deep-frying is an important cooking method, something similar to batter will have evolved to fulfil this role, although the ingredients may differ substantially from those used in Europe. Japanese tempura recipes call for various combinations of flour, egg (or egg yolk alone), and water; Chinese deep-fried recipes for wheat flour, cornflour, and water; and the Indian pakora, a type of vegetable fritter, uses a batter of chickpea flour and water.

In the USA, the meaning of 'batter' extends to some thicker mixtures such as those for cake and for spoon bread (sometimes called 'batter bread').

More generally, cooked in a thin layer in the bottom of a frying pan, a batter makes pancakes or crêpes. Poured in a thicker layer in a large tin, and baked in the oven, it becomes Yorkshire pudding.

However, despite the fame of this last item in its savoury version, most batter puddings are sweet. One example is the French clafoutis, which contains fruit. Fruit is also an ingredient in many of the English batter puddings, of which Dorothy Hartley gives an impressive range, from medieval to modern times. Some are boiled or steamed, for example the Gotham pudding from the little town of that name in Nottingham, which incorporates slices of candied peel and, after being steamed, is to be served 'with cowslip wine and sugar'. Another steamed batter pudding belongs to Tiverton in Devon, incorporates ginger and other spices as well as candied lemon rind, is served with butter and sugar, and 'should be eaten at once while light and spongy'. However, many, e.g. Kentish cherry batter pudding, are baked.

Tewkesbury (or Welsh) saucer batters are small baked puddings made by quickly baking two saucerfuls of batter, putting fruit on one and inverting the other on top of it to make a lid. These ingenious snack meals, 'ready by the time the kettle boils' for tea, may be unique to the Tewkesbury area and other fruit-picking districts. However, their small size is echoed in small baked batter puddings made elsewhere: for example, the American popover, and the Austrian *Pfitzkauf* ('puff up') which is eaten as a dessert with fruit.

Beeton, Isabella: (1836–65) author of the most famous cookery book in the English language, does not correspond at all to the general impression which people have of her. The sheer size and scope and authoritative air of this book, *Beeton's Book of Household Management*, have caused people to imagine a matronly figure, in middle age, if not older, perhaps looking somewhat like the standard image of Queen Victoria, during whose reign Mrs Beeton lived.

In fact, she was a beautiful young woman, married to a bright and enterprising young publisher, who started at the age of 21 to produce material for her husband's *English Woman's Domestic Magazine*, including the collection of vast numbers of recipes and information about how to run a household. She was only 25 years old when her work appeared in book form, and only 28 when she died (of puerperal fever, contracted after giving birth to her fourth child – and having lost the first two in infancy).

Her book, in its first edition, was a triumph of organization, common sense and kitchen skills. Mrs Beeton had borrowed from her great predecessor, Eliza Acton, the innovative method of setting out recipes in a standard way, with appropriate brevity but also with the requisite details. And she was well served by her friends and by contributors to the magazine for which she worked. Yet, whatever benefits of this nature she enjoyed, the compilation and editing of what was the greatest work on cookery and household management in the 19th century called for an extraordinary talent. This she displayed, with occasional flashes of a pretty wit, to lighten what might otherwise have seemed too didactic an approach to her readers. Didactic, of course, she had to be because the task she had set herself was to instruct both mistress and housekeeper in all aspects of housekeeping, while supplying background information on the natural history of foodstuffs (a feature in which she anticipated developments which in the main did not take place until a hundred years later) and explaining points of etiquette and wrapping up the whole package with advice on lifestyles and morals which was intended to ensure that her readers approached their tasks in the appropriate frame of mind. To do all this required an almost military approach ('As with the commander of an army . . . so is it with the mistress of a house,' she wrote) and a decisiveness which would ensure that readers were not left bemused by too many alternatives or vague instructions. After all, their days would hardly be long enough to cope with their manifold tasks, even if they completely eschewed the 'faffing around' which messes up the day for so many people. Mrs Beeton recommended early rising ('one of the most essential qualities'). She noted with approval that Lord Chatham gave this advice: 'I would have inscribed on the curtains of your bed, and the walls of your chamber, "If you do not rise early, you can make progress in nothing."'

However, a great book such as hers could not be based solely on such exhortations to readers, comprehensive scope, good organization, and a clear style. The some-thing more which was necessary to make it great was that intangible quality which is hard to pin down but which radiates almost palpably from the finest cookery books, an emanation which tells the readers that the author really knows what she is about.

Given that her book merits such high praise it is all the more unfortunate that its later history was on the whole a sad one. Sam Beeton ran into financial difficulties in 1867, while seriously ill and still suffering from the shock of bereavement. He relinquished all his copyrights, including his late wife's book, to the publishing firm Ward, Lock & Tyler. Elizabeth David has chronicled what happened thereafter. To begin with, the new pub-lishers were content to reprint and to produce abridged volumes. However, a new and considerably changed edition came out in 1888, containing much which Mrs

Beeton had not written and would not have written. In 1906 there followed a completely revised edition, with the cookery sections re-edited by a well-known chef and author, C. Herman Senn. Elizabeth David comments that, although this carried the book considerably further away from the down-to-earth approach of the original author, grafting on to it 'refined little things in dariole moulds' etc., such as Edwardian professional chefs delighted to produce, and adding 'other laughable little items' which left Mrs Beeton's reputation vulnerable to critical scorn, the Senn edition was 'a wonderful and beautiful book' and was still a coherent whole.

It was at this point that references by Sam Beeton to his 'late wife' dropped out of the book, leaving the unwary to suppose that she might still be alive and tendering her advice; and from then on it was downhill all the way until eventually, by the 1960s, the revised book did not contain a single recipe as written by the author. Fortunately, two other publishers subsequently produced facsimile reprints of the first (1861) edition, so that those who would like to savour Isabella Beeton's recipes and homilies directly from the original source may easily do so.

Blackberry: is a name which usually refers to the common European blackberry, *Rubus fruticosus*, also known as bramble; but it is also a collective name for a large group of fruits in the same genus which grow throughout the cooler parts of the world, particularly in upland and northern regions.

There are said to be over 2,000 varieties of blackberry, counting both the frequent and naturally occurring hybrids and the cultivars.

The genus *Rubus* also includes raspberries. The untrained eye cannot always distinguish between a blackberry and a raspberry, since the shapes and sizes of the fruit, leaves, and thorns vary, and there are both red blackberries and black raspberries. However, when a blackberry is picked, it comes off the plant with its receptacle, the solid centre to which the druplets (the round, juicy parts) are attached. When a raspberry is picked, the cluster of druplets comes away from the receptacle, which remains as a hard, white cone on the stem. A good blackberry has druplets which are large in relation to the hard part.

Blackberries are more highly esteemed in Britain and N. Europe than in other European countries. During their season they are commonly gathered and eaten fresh, as they keep for only a short time; or they may be used in desserts such as the British blackberry and apple pie. They are sometimes preserved by bottling but lose much of their evanescent flavour. They make an excellent jelly but a somewhat pippy jam. Tea made from blackberry leaves is a traditional cure for indigestion and is believed to purify the blood.

In Britain it used to be considered unlucky to pick blackberries after a certain date, sometimes Michaelmas (29 September) but with regional variants, as in Warwickshire, 12 October, the day of the traditional 'Mop' or hiring fair. Later than this, the devil was believed to have stamped or spat on the berries.

Blackbird: *Turdus merula*, a familiar European songbird, which ranges from the southern parts of Norway and Sweden down to the Mediterranean.

The English nursery rhyme about four-and-twenty blackbirds baked in a pie might suggest that large blackbird pies were once common fare; but since 'when the pie was open'd, the birds began to sing,' the allusion must be to the medieval conceits known as subtleties, which often featured such surprises. However, blackbirds were eaten in the Middle Ages and the 17th century and even later (see, for example, a recipe for Blackbird pie given by Mrs Beeton). In a few regions of continental Europe blackbirds are still used in pies or to make terrines.

Bone marrow: the soft, nutritious substance found in the internal cavities of animal bones, especially the shin bones of oxen and calves. The French term is *moelle*.

The spinal marrow of oxen and calves is sometimes known as 'ox pith'. Pieces of it, or of the same thing from sheep, are commonly called *amourettes* in French.

Marrow was formerly a prized delicacy, to be cooked and served in its bone from which it would be removed with a special silver marrow scoop.

Dorothy Hartley provides charming drawings which show how marrow bones were baked in Georgian times, with a small paste crust sealing the cut end, and how they were boiled if the marrow was to be served on hot buttered toast. She says that in the Middle Ages marrow was a well-loved food, mainly used for sweet dishes. Later, in the time of Queen Victoria, marrow was considered to be a man's food and 'unladylike', although Queen Victoria herself apparently ate marrow toast for tea every day. Dorothy Hartley comments that this 'was certainly not correct diet for her plump Majesty'. She does, however, further comment that: 'Marrow is the most liked and digestible fat, and should be given to children and invalids who require building up.'

Sheila Hutchins, writing in 1971, mentioned that baked marrow bones were 'still served hot in a napkin at City dinners and a few old-fashioned public houses' in London. More remarkably, she gave two recipes for marrow pudding, one of which was the family pudding of Sir Watkin Williams-Wynn. According to Sir Watkin, the recipe dated from the mid-18th century and the pudding was still, when Sheila Hutchins interviewed him, being 'served regularly with hot jam sauce at his table and at that of the dowager Lady Watkin Williams-Wynn' (at the age of 95). The preferred jam was raspberry jam.

Brandy snaps: crisp, lacy baked items which stand on the frontier between biscuits, wafers, and sugar confectionery. They are made from butter, sugar, and golden syrup, mixed with flour, and flavoured with ginger, brandy (sometimes) and lemon juice. Teaspoonfuls of the mixture are dropped on to trays and baked gently. During baking the mixture spreads into a thin sheet; this is lifted off the tray with a spatula while warm, and rolled round a wooden spoon handle to give a hollow cylinder. When cold, it may be filled with whipped cream.

On the question whether brandy is or is not used (which seems to make no difference to the flavour) the delightfully ponderous comments by Garrett (*c.*1898) are relevant:

These delights of our youth were probably originally made with a Brandy flavouring as one of their ingredients; but with that lack of discriminative taste peculiar to uneducated palates, the presence of the Brandy flavour was not sufficiently appreciated to render its presence essential to the success of the manufacture; hence, as the 'snaps' could be made cheaper without Brandy, and yielded more sweets for the same money, the spiritous prefix became but a name.

Brandy snaps are traditional English 'fairings', treats to buy at the fair, and are sometimes sold flat rather than rolled. Black treacle was used in earlier versions.

Brawn: a moulded, jellied cold meat preparation, usually made from a pig's head, but also sometimes from a sheep or ox head or, in some parts of Britain, rabbit. The meat is lightly cured in brine, then boiled until it can be trimmed and boned. The essential feature of brawn is that it is made of gelatinous meat, such as is furnished by a head, so that when the meat is cooked the rich broth extracted from it can be boiled down to make the jelly in which the coarsely chopped meat is set. Brawn is usually moulded in a cylindrical shape, like a cheese;

hence the American name 'head cheese' and the French *fromage de tête*.

In medieval Britain brawn was made from wild boar, then abundant. Indeed, the term had originally meant the flesh of wild boar. Brawn, in the narrower sense which the word acquired, was valued for its fatty rich quality, and was eaten at Christmas, a tradition which persisted to modern times. In those days it was not made into a moulded jelly, but was kept in a pot, covered with a pickling liquor of ale, verjuice, and salt, from which it was taken out to serve. It was often made into a rich pottage or sliced and served in a thick, sweet wine sauce. By the 14th century it had acquired its traditional accompaniment of a mild mustard sauce.

By the 16th century the British wild boar had become rare, and pigs, specially fattened on whey, were used instead. In the 17th century, when the potting of meats was newly fashionable, brawn became a potted preparation, baked in wine in its pot, then drained and filled up with butter. From the 18th century on it assumed its modern form of a jellied product.

Early brawns were heavily spiced, but the plainer tastes of the 18th century reduced the amount of flavouring, and nowadays only a small amount of sage or other herbs, and perhaps a little lemon juice, are usual.

Cheddar: the most famous and widespread hard cheese in the world, takes its name from the village of Cheddar, by Cheddar Gorge in the English county of Somerset. However, the name has now come to indicate technique of cheese-making rather than a place of origin, for Cheddar cheese is now made not only in other parts of the British Isles but also in other continents.

'Cheddaring', which is just one step in the many which lead to the final product, refers to the cutting of the curd into slabs which are piled upon each other to produce a smooth mass; it is not a term which would be used by any but cheese-makers.

Cheddar cheese is made from whole cow's milk and, in its traditional form, matured for a considerable time – a year to eighteen months if it is to be savoured at its best. To produce such cheeses obviously requires a considerable investment of time and effort, all the more so since the Cheddar normally is and always has been a big cheese. Cheddars used to be called corporation cheeses in Somerset, because they were made by all the dairies of a parish putting their milk together. The results were impressive. One of the most weighty contributions to Queen Victoria's wedding celebrations was a Cheddar cheese over 9' (2.7 m) in diameter and registering 1,250 lb (567 kg) on the scales. Two villages had combined to make the monster.

However, small quantities of milk left over from making the big Cheddars were used to make small ones, in the form of a little round loaf called a truckle; and it is still possible in the west of England to buy farmhouse truckles which have an excellent flavour, full and 'nutty' as a Cheddar should be, and with the firm but creamy texture and the pale glow which are the marks of real quality.

Such cheeses, made by small producers in limited

quantities, have qualities far surpassing mass-produced versions. Nonetheless, many of the latter represent excellent value for those who seek an unpretentious cheese which goes well with bread and ale, keeps well, and melts satisfactorily when heated.

Cheshire: is thought to be Britain's oldest named cheese. It is mentioned in the Domesday Book at the end of the 11th century, but was probably made long before then.

Good Cheshire must (unlike Cheddar) be made in its region of origin; this is around Chester, the county town of Cheshire. The flavour of the cheese depends on the salty, marl and sandstone, grazing land along the River Dee and its tributaries; also no doubt on the cattle, those same cattle which, in Charles Kingsley's sad poem, Mary was invited to call home across the sands of Dee.

Cheshire is a large, hard-pressed, drum-shaped, whole milk cheese typically weighing 30 kg (70 lb). The texture is crumbly but not moist, and the flavour mild and slightly acid. It was formerly made in early-, medium-, and late-ripening varieties, of which the last, aged for as long as 10 months, was considered best. Now, however, it has been standardized at a medium, six-month, ripening time.

In its natural state Cheshire is a pale cream colour. However, it is often coloured orange with annatto (since the end of the 18th century, before which carrot juice was used), a practice which probably originated as a means of giving the cheese a rich look, in rivalry with other, deeper-coloured cheeses. There is also a highly regarded blue Cheshire, locally known as 'green fade' cheese.

Gerard (1633) records the preference for rennet made from lady's bedstraw in making Cheshire cheese, 'especially about Namptwich [Nantwich] where the best Cheese is made'. This practice seems to have died out by the end of the 18th century.

Giant Cheshire cheeses have been recorded. In 1909 an order for 20, each to weigh 300 lb (136 kg), was executed with success. But this exploit seems to have been surpassed by cheese-makers in the town of Cheshire, Massachusetts, who established a tradition of giving mammoth cheeses to an incoming president of the United States, and whose cheese for President Jackson, after it had stood in state for weeks at the White House while Democrats ate their fill from it, still left the floor a foot deep in fragments.

The French and Germans make a cooking cheese called 'Chester', originally intended to resemble Cheshire (which enjoyed an international reputation long before Cheddar did, and was mentioned in the first printed cheese book, of 1477). But, nowadays at least, 'Chester' bears only a slight resemblance to its original.

Chitterling(s): the small intestine, or part thereof, of a pig (or, less often, another animal – Hannah Glasse (1747) refers to calf's chitterling), especially when prepared for use as food. Jane Grigson remarks that 'The unforgettable name is of unknown derivation, but appears in the 13th century in dog-latin form in a description of women washing "chitterlingis" down by the waterside.' The form 'chitlings' is also in use.

Chitterlings have a twofold use in the making of sausages such as andouilles and andouillettes; chopped up, they provide an ingredient for the filling, while they are also used to furnish casings.

Apart from sausages, there are only a few dishes in which chitterlings are a main ingredient. In England, chopped chitterlings were used in the 16th century in a kind of white pudding and a chitterling pie was known in England in the 18th century. Indeed, C. Anne Wilson quotes a passage from Ellis (1750) which emphasizes the need to wash them and scour them with salt very thoroughly, and continues thus: 'Others boil sage in their water to take off their hogoo [*haut goût*, i.e. strong flavour], for the preparation of chitterlings will prove the cleanliness or sluttishness of a housewife as much as any meat whatsoever will.' If dealing with chitterlings was a kind of hallmark for hygiene in the kitchen, their use must have been common.

Although chitterlings have largely dropped from view in Britain, their use continues in those countries where all forms of offal are eaten, even though cooks there may have no precisely equivalent term. (There are many recipes which call for intestines, a more general term which would often include chitterlings.)

Christmas pudding: the rich culmination of a long process of development of 'plum puddings' which can be traced back to the early 15th century. The first types were not specifically associated with Christmas. Like early mince pies, they contained meat, of which a token remains in the use of suet. The original form, plum pottage, was made from chopped beef or mutton, onions and perhaps other root vegetables, and dried fruit, thickened with bread crumbs, and flavoured with wine, herbs, and spices. As the name suggests, it was a fairly liquid preparation: this was before the invention of the pudding cloth made large puddings feasible. As was usual with such dishes, it was served at the beginning of a meal. When new kinds of dried fruit became available in Britain, first raisins, then prunes in the 16th century, they were added. The name 'plum' refers to a prune; but it soon came to mean any dried fruit.

In the 16th century variants were made with white meat such as chicken or veal; and gradually the meat came to be omitted, to be replaced by suet. The root vegetables also disappeared, although even now Christmas pudding often still includes a token carrot. The rich dish was served on feast days such as All Saints' Day, Christmas, and New Year's Day. By the 1670s, it was particularly associated with Christmas and called 'Christmas pottage'. The old plum pottage continued to be made into the 18th century, and both versions were still served as a filling first course rather than as a dessert.

Not all plum puddings were rich, festive, or cere-monial. Plum duff, essentially a suet pudding with less fruit and other enrichment, remained popular for centuries.

Even before Christmas pudding had attained its

modern form, its consumption on Christmas Day had been banned by Oliver Cromwell. This was not simply a sign of his Puritan attitudes. The Christian Church everywhere was conscious that Christmas was merely a veneer of the old Celtic winter solstice fire festival celebrating the 'rebirth' of the sun after the shortest day, 21 or 22 December. This is still frankly celebrated in the Orkneys with the rite of Up Helly A, when a ship is burnt. Signs of paganism keep emerging: for example, the Yule log, a huge log which is kept burning for all twelve days of the festival, and is still commemorated in the traditional French log-shaped Christmas cake. Other relics are the candles on the Christmas tree (imported from Germany in the time of Prince Albert), and the flaming pudding itself. There had been a similar official attitude in Scotland towards the consumption of the black bun on Twelfth Night.

What currently counts as the traditional Christmas pudding recipe has been more or less established since the 19th century. Usual ingredients are: suet; brown sugar (not always); raisins; sultanas; currants; candied peel; bread crumbs; eggs; spices such as cinammon, nutmeg, and cloves, or allspice or mixed spice; and alcohol (e.g. stout, rum, brandy). Optional ingredients include flour, fresh orange or lemon peel, grated carrot or apple, almonds. The result is a remarkably solid pudding which has to be boiled for many hours then preferably left to mature for up to a year and reboiled on the day. A large pudding resists this treatment better than small ones – though few are as large as the one made in Devon in 1819, which weighed over 400 kg (900 lb).

The pudding is traditionally served with rum or brandy butter (US hard sauce) made from butter, sugar and spirit. It is topped with a sprig of holly and set alight with rum or another spirit. This part of the tradition is still widely observed, but recipes for the pudding itself have been evolving in the direction of something lighter and more digestible.

The shape of the pudding is traditionally spherical, from being tied up in a floured pudding cloth. Most modern puddings are made in a basin covered with layers of foil and greaseproof paper.

Comfit: an archaic English word for an item of confectionery consisting of a seed, or nut coated in several layers of sugar, equivalent to the French dragée. In England these small, hard sugar sweets were often made with caraway seeds, known for sweetening the breath (hence 'kissing comfits'). Up to a dozen coats of syrup were needed before the seeds were satisfactorily encrusted. Comfits were eaten as sweets, and also used in other sweet dishes: for example seed cake was made with caraway comfits rather than loose caraway seeds as in the 19th century.

Confectioners as early as the 17th century recognized that by varying the proportions of sugar in the syrup they could change the final texture, making 'pearled' comfits or 'crisp and ragged' comfits.

The word 'comfit' remained in use in English up until the 20th century: Alice, of *Alice in Wonderland*, has a box of comfits in her pocket. During the 20th century, however, it has become obsolete, and the confectionery produced by this method is now known under individual names – sugar almonds, hundreds and thousands, gobstoppers are a few examples.

Coventry godcakes: have now, according to Laura Mason, become extinct. They were small, triangular sweet pastries filled with mixed dried fruit. Flaky or puff pastry could be used.

Coventry children formerly gave these to their god-parents at Easter. The triangular shape may be a reference to the Trinity.

Crumpet: a type of thick, perforated pancake made from a yeast-leavened batter containing milk. Crumpets are cooked on a lightly greased griddle, confined in ring moulds. Since the 19th century, the leaven in the batter has been boosted by a little bicarbonate of soda just before cooking. Batter consistency is important: the characteristic mass of tiny holes will not develop if it is too thick.

Crumpets are only turned briefly on the griddle, the underside taking on a pale gold colour and smooth surface, while the top remains pallid. This is intentional as they undergo a second cooking by toasting after which they are spread lavishly with butter on the holey side. Dorothy Hartley says that crumpets may 'vary locally from large brownish dinner-plate size made with an admixture of brown flour in some mountain districts, to small, rather thick, very holey crumpets made in the Midlands'.

The earliest published recipe for crumpets of the kind known now is from Elizabeth Raffald (1769). Ayto, in an entertaining essay, discusses a possible 14th-century ancestor, the crompid cake, and the buckwheat griddle cakes (called crumpit) which appeared from the late 17th century onwards. He also illuminates the sexual connotation of crumpet, pointing out that it is now used of sexually attractive men as well as women, and that there was an analogous use of muffin (for women) in 19th-century Canadian English.

It seems clear enough that there is a connection with Welsh *crempog* (pancake) and Breton *krampoch* (buckwheat pancake).

Reading the collection of crumpet, muffin and pikelet recipes made by Elizabeth David underlines the confusion of method and terminology between these three forms of yeasted pancake cooked on a griddle. A consensus might be that crumpets are made with a thinner batter than muffins, hence the need to confine them in rings (though this was not invariable), and hence too the holes in the top. Muffins are baked thicker, thick enough to be pulled asunder after toasting which crumpets would never be. Pikelets seems a northern usage – though perhaps originally Welsh if the proposed derivation from *bara pyglyd* ('pitchy bread') is accepted. Again the consensus is that the pikelet is near identical to a crumpet, though the batter is thinner still and baked without a ring on the griddle, thus much more like a yeasted pancake.

Devil: a culinary term which according to the *NSOED* first appeared as a noun in the 18th century, and then in the early 19th century as a verb meaning to cook something with fiery hot spices or condiments. Theodora FitzGibbon remarks, however, that 'Boswell, Dr Johnson's biographer, frequently refers to partaking of a dish of "devilled bones" for supper', which suggests an earlier use. The term was presumably adopted because of the connection between the devil and the excessive heat in Hell.

Devilled bones and devilled kidneys are just two examples of the dishes in this category, which could be referred to as 'devils'. Writing about this noun, Fitz-Gibbon distinguishes between brown devils, wet devils, and white devils, explaining the differences between these. An earlier authority, Dallas (1877) in *Kettner's Book of the Table*, had stated that devils were of two kinds, the dry and the wet, but had also commented:

It is the great fault of all devilry that it knows no bounds. A moderate devil is almost a contradiction in terms; and yet it is quite certain that if a devil is not moderate he destroys the palate, and ought to have no place in cookery, the business of which is to tickle, not to annihilate, the sense of taste.

The dilemma thus stated may have proved insoluble, for devilling has fallen out of fashion.

A certain parallel exists in France in the form of dishes 'à la diable'.

One of the British savouries which was popular for

a time bore the name Devils on horseback and consisted of prunes stuffed with chutney, rolled up in rashers of bacon, placed on buttered bread and sprinkled with grated cheese, and cooked under the grill. The absence of cayenne pepper or other hot condiments suggests that in this instance the word 'devil' was introduced as a counterpart to 'angel' in Angels on horseback rather than in the sense described above.

Digby, Sir Kenelm: (1603–65) an adventurous and romantic figure of 17th-century England whose eccentric and posthumously published recipe book has earned him the interest and esteem of food historians.

His father, a convert to the Roman Catholic Church, died when he was still a boy; and it was a Protestant uncle who took him, at age 14 and for two years, to Spain, where he began his lifelong habit of collecting medical and culinary recipes. Later, at Oxford, he studied under a famous mathematician and astrologer, and also fell in love, with a notorious beauty, Venetia Stanley. Opposing the match, his mother packed him off on a three-year Grand Tour of France and Italy, but he married Venetia when he returned and the marriage lasted happily for eight years, until Venetia's sudden death in 1633.

After Venetia's death, Digby had a spell as an Anglican, but then reverted to being a Catholic and spent some time, after the execution of King Charles, as a spokesman seeking toleration for the Catholics in England. This and other politico-religious activities were accompanied by activity in the newly formed Royal Society and by much writing. He wrote prolifically, including works of literary criticism and philosophy. However, his most lasting work has proved to be one which he never saw in print. This was his collection of recipes, assembled after his death and published by his laboratory assistant Hartman for his own profit under the title *The Closet of the Eminently Learned Sir Kenelme Digbie Kt. Opened: Whereby is Discovered Several ways for making of Metheglin, Sider, Cherry-Wine, &c. Together with Excellent Directions for Cookery: As also for Preserving, Conserving, Candying, &c.*

This book begins with 106 recipes for mead, metheglyn, and other drinks mostly based on fermented honey and herbs. Some had been contributed by sundry friends and professional cooks, others were the fruits of Digby's own research. They are followed by possets, syllabubs, and creams, and by soups and gruels for health and nourishment. There follows a somewhat jumbled collection of savoury dishes. Recipes for fruit preserves, tonic sweetmeats (including the remarkable 'Cordial Tablets', whose worth has been proved in the late 20th century), cosmetic cures, and a perfume for tobacco round off the collection. Because it has an engagingly amateur, yet learned, air about it and reflects the attractive enthusiasm of the author, the book, which has been twice reprinted in the 20th century, seems sure to continue finding appreciative readers.

Dock pudding: a mixture of 'dock' (i.e. bistort, *Polygonum bistorta*), oatmeal, onions, and nettles, thickened with oatmeal and boiled together. There are those who profess to love it, and those who loathe it. It tastes something like a cross between spinach and asparagus. Once cooked, it is fried by the dollop or slice in plenty of old-fashioned, real, bacon fat to counteract the strong taste and green slimy consistency. When it has a crisp, fatty, salty outside, it is more palatable.

Dock pudding has become synonymous with Calderdale (in W. Yorkshire), especially Mytholmroyd, Hebden Bridge, and Todmorden, ever since 1971. It was in that year that the first competition to find the World's Champion Dock Pudding Makers was held there. However, dock pudding is by no means unique to Calderdale. The truth is that bistort has been used in many similar pottages and puddings for centuries, in many areas of England and S. Scotland.

Up to the 17th century, oatmeal pottage (poddige, porridge) was a universal food in Britain, eaten by rich and poor alike. It was often enlivened, both for flavour and food value, with green herbs such as daisy, tansy, dandelion, nettles, kale, etc. But at Easter time, it was invested with a special significance, partly as a seasonal ritual, partly as a vital spring blood cleanser and anti-scorbutic. (Up to the 19th century, many people had scurvy by February because of a lack of green stuff in winter.) The Easter connection of bistort pudding is reflected in various local names for bistort: passion dock or patience dock (from Passiontide), pash-docken (Littondale), Easter mangiant, Easter giant, Easter ledger, etc. It is called passion or patience dock in Yorkshire, Derbyshire, and N. England, and known mainly as patience dock in Cheshire and Lancashire.

Dumpling: Early dumplings were probably balls of bread dough taken from the batch used to make bread. However, people soon began to make dumplings from other ingredients, e.g. suet or white bread. By 1747 Hannah Glasse could give no fewer than eight recipes for dumplings, of which two were for 'hard' dumplings made from plain flour and water, 'best boiled with a good piece of beef'; two were for apple dumplings; and others were for Norfolk dumplings, yeast dumplings, white bread dumplings, and suet dumplings. When she indicated size, she usually said 'as big as a turkey's egg'.

Norfolk is the chief dumpling county of Britain, but the history of its honourable (and plain) dumplings has been obscured by French intervention. The story told by Dumas in his *Grand Dictionnaire de cuisine* that the Duke of Norfolk was fond of dumplings, and that they are named after him, is wrong, as is the recipe Dumas gives. Indeed, the recipe is so wildly wrong that it looks as though Dumas was the victim of a practical joker when he visited England, possibly the same person who told him that Yermouth [*sic*], home of bloaters, was in Ireland.

A good description of how Norfolk dumplings were and are made is given by Mrs Arthur Webb (*c.*1935):

The farmer's wife very skilfully divided a pound of dough (remember, just ordinary bread dough) into four pieces. These she weighed, and so cleverly had she gauged the size that they weighed approximately 4 oz each. She kneaded, and rolled them in a very little flour until they were quite round, then put them on a plate and slipped them into a large saucepan containing fast-boiling water. The saucepan lid was put back immediately, and then, when the water came to the boil once more, 15 minutes' rapid boiling was allowed for the dumplings.

Dumplings in Norfolk are not a sweet. They are a very substantial part of what might be the meat course, or they might serve as a meat substitute. In the villages I found that they were sometimes put into a very large pot and boiled on top of the greens; then they are called 'swimmer'.

Eliza Acton (1845), apparently referring to Norfolk dumplings, specified several accompaniments: wine sauce, raspberry vinegar, or sweetened melted butter with a little vinegar.

Suffolk dumplings, unlike those of Norfolk, are made of flour and water, without yeast. (Eliza Acton recommended adding milk to make a thick batter.) They are steamed or rapidly boiled, so that they rise well. They may be eaten with meat gravy, or with butter or syrup. They often include currants if intended as a sweet dish.

Oatmeal dumplings are common in N. Britain, where oats are widely grown. Derbyshire dumplings, relatively small, are made from equal amounts of wheat flour and oatmeal, with beef dripping and onion; to be added to a beef stew half an hour before serving.

Eccles cakes: small English cakes similar to Banbury cakes, except that they are normally round in shape and the filling has fewer ingredients; currants, wheat flour, brown sugar, butter and vegetable fat, milk, and salt are standard.

The cakes take their name from the small town on the outskirts of Manchester where they were first made and named. Mrs Raffald, herself from Manchester and the author of one of the best cookery books of the 18th century, had given a recipe for 'sweet patties' which may well have been the confections from which Eccles cakes evolved. Mrs Raffald's filling included meat (from a calf's foot), apple, candied peel, and currants, an assemblage compatible with what the term mincemeat used to mean.

The first mention of Eccles cakes by name seems likely to have occurred at the end of the 18th century when a certain James Birch was making them. An apprentice of his, William Bradburn, had set up a rival operation by about 1813. Evelyn Vigeon (1993), in her brilliant and comprehensive history of these cakes, describes the confrontation:

James Birch advertised that he was the original Eccles cake maker *removed from across the way*, while William Bradburn retaliated with an advertisement claiming that his shop was *the only old original Eccles Cakes Shop. Never removed*. This rivalry was to the advantage of both manufacturers over the following century since visitors would often buy cakes from both shops to be sure they had indeed tasted the *original* one.

The same author traces the later history of these and other Eccles cake establishments, and provides details of some recipes published in the 19th century. She believes that early Eccles cakes may well have differed from those known now, both in shape (some at least were sold cut in squares) and the nature of the pastry (puff or flaky pastry is now used), and ingredients for the filling. She points out that the fact that Eccles cakes were being exported abroad by 1818 suggests very good keeping qualities, 'so they may well have included spirits such as brandy and rum in the same way as the nineteenth century Banbury cake'.

Chorley cakes are a variation of Eccles cakes, usually somewhat plainer.

Eve's pudding: is the modern name of a baked pudding with a lower layer of chopped apples and an upper one of a sponge mixture flavoured with lemon and vanilla. This is really a descendant of a grander pudding of the 18th century, Duke of Cumberland's pudding, which was boiled. The apples were therefore inside rather than underneath. The surrounding pudding was made of a very highly egged suet mixture. It was served with melted butter, wine, and sugar.

The name 'Mother Eve's Pudding' appears in a 19th-century verse recipe for a boiled pudding which is like the Duke's, but without suet and with currants. The name of the Duke, who was the bloody victor of Culloden, may have been suppressed to suit Victorian sensibilities; but the anonymous poet is none too tender-hearted: 'Six ounces of bread (let your maid eat the crust . . .).'

Dunfillan pudding is a Scottish pudding, similar to Eve's pudding but made with blackberries instead of apples.

Faggot: in Britain, is a term for a simplified form of sausage, easier and quicker to make at home than a proper one. A mixture of pork offal – liver, lungs, spleen, etc. – fat, breadcrumbs, onions, and flavourings to taste is parcelled in squares of caul (the fatty membrane around the intestines). The parcels are packed into a tin and baked, and may be eaten hot or cold. Faggots have also long been made commercially: it was an accident with a batch of faggots at a shop in Pudding Lane which started the Great Fire of London in 1666.

Since faggots are made from cheap ingredients they have always been a popular food of the poor, especially in the north of England. They are also called 'savoury ducks' because of the resemblance of the little packages to small birds. The same idea is behind the name of the French equivalent, *caillettes* (little quails) or (more commonly now) *gayettes*. These are made of liver, fat bacon, and sometimes sweetbreads or other offal or lean pork, with garlic, sometimes shallots, and herbs and spices – but not with breadcrumbs or other cereal. They are baked in the same way as faggots, sometimes interspersed with tomatoes.

Fish and chips: may fairly be said to constitute one of the national dishes of England (and Scotland), but does not have a very long history. The combination, in its familiar form, is thought to date back to the 1860s, in Lancashire or in London. However, the two component parts had existed separately for more than half a century before then, and it would be a rash historian who would deny the possibility that they had joined forces, somewhere, somewhat sooner.

Fried fish, sold in pieces, cold, must have been established as a standard street food in London by the 1840s or earlier. As Picton remarks, Dickens mentions a 'fried fish warehouse' in *Oliver Twist*, published in instalments 1837–9. At that time the fish was sold with a chunk of bread. Mayhew, who wrote his famous survey of London Labour and the London Poor in the 1850s and early 1860s, painted a lively portrait of a fried fish seller, stating that there were about 300 of them in London, and that one of them had been in the trade for 17 years. As Claudia Roden observes, there was a strong Jewish tradition of frying fish in batter and eating it cold. And it was 'fried fish in the Jewish fashion' which Thomas Jefferson discovered when he came to London and which was included in the first Jewish cookbook in English. Roden also remarks that the National Federation of Fish Friers presented in 1968 a plaque to Malin's of Bow in London's East End as the oldest fried fish and chips establishment still in business; and speculates that the combination represented a coming together in London (or wherever) of E. European Jewish immigrants (for the fish) and Irish immigrants (for the potato).

Chips had an earlier history, probably from the late 18th century. However, potatoes as street food in the early 19th century mostly took the form of hot baked potatoes and these were a seasonal trade. It is not clear when chips achieved real popularity, nor whether it was in London or the mill towns of Lancashire that this happened.

The marriage of fish and chips, wherever it was consummated, gained popularity swiftly and spread, for example to Ireland; Darina Allen says that it was Italian immigrants (who had become prominent in the fish and chip trade in Scotland) who brought the combination over to Ireland and who still have a secure hold on the business in Dublin. The number of fish and chip establishments grew steadily until the Second World War. Although variations on their standard fare, and various gimmicks, were often introduced, the basics never changed: fish (usually cod, haddock, skate, dogfish); malt vinegar; salt; perhaps a piece of lemon. There was also the traditional wrapping of newspaper, but that was already being phased out on hygienic grounds in the 1960s.

Fruit cake: a British speciality, is a close, rich, heavy cake made by the creaming method, raised with baking powder and beaten egg. Up to half the weight of the finished cake may consist of dried fruit. In earlier centuries it was called plum (or plumb) cake, 'plum' denoting all kinds of dried fruits. Today the name plum cake survives (in the English form) on the mainland of Europe, though here it often means a sadly dry product without much fruit.

Fruit cakes are used as part of celebrations, such as weddings. They also loom large among Christmas foods and may make an appearance at christenings and birthdays. Many families have their own favourite recipes. Decoration is important; festive fruit cakes are usually topped with marzipan and covered with royal icing suitably embellished with piping, cut paper, and little figures.

Lighter cakes, made with less fruit, to be eaten at tea-time or for snacks, include Genoa cake (not to be confused with génoise). Dundee cake is a medium-weight species of fruit cake.

The fruit in these cakes may be any or all of currants, raisins, sultanas, and candied peel. Candied fruits, particularly cherries, are usually added, as are ground almonds.

Alcohol, usually brandy, is sometimes mixed into the batter for rich fruit cakes before baking. Some prefer to add it afterwards, by making small holes in the base of the cake with a skewer and dripping in a little liquid. This process may be repeated several times, as a fruit cake keeps for months when correctly stored; it is quite normal for it to be made well in advance of the event for which it is required, and most people consider it improved by keeping.

The fruit cake as known today cannot date back much beyond the Middle Ages. It was only in the 13th century that dried fruits began to arrive in Britain, from Portugal and the E. Mediterranean. Lightly fruited breads were probably more common than anything resembling the modern fruit cake during the Middle Ages. Early versions of the rich fruit cake, such as Scottish black bun dating from the late Middle Ages, were luxuries for special occasions.

Fruit cakes have been used for celebrations since at least the early 18th century when 'bride cakes' and 'plumb cakes', descended from enriched bread recipes, became cookery standards. The relationship between fruit breads and fruit cakes is obvious in early recipes, such as those given by Eliza Smith (1753) which include yeast.

Prodigious quantities of ingredients were required. Relatively modest plum cake recipes given by Eliza Smith called for 4 lb (1.8 kg) of flour to be mixed with sugar, spice, eggs, sack, cream, currants, and candied lemon, orange, and citron. Her 'Great cake' required among other things 13 lb (6 kg) of currants, 5 pints (2.8 litres) of cream and 4 lb of butter, 20 egg yolks, and 3 pints of yeast. Surprisingly little sugar was called for: only 1.5 lb (700 g). This probably reflects the cookery practices of the late 17th century, as Smith wrote her book at the end of her career.

Making a rich fruit cake in an 18th-century kitchen was a major undertaking. The ingredients had to be carefully prepared. Fruit was washed, dried, and stoned if necessary; sugar, cut from loaves, had to be pounded and sieved; butter washed in water and rinsed in rose-water. Eggs were beaten for a long time, half an hour being commonly directed. Yeast, or 'barm' from fermenting beer, had to be coaxed into life. Finally, the cook had to cope with the temperamental wood-fired baking ovens of that time. No wonder these cakes acquired such mystique.

By the mid-18th century the use of yeast as a cake leavener was dying out. In the 19th it seems to have been more or less forgotten, except for regional specialities such as bara brith. Mrs Beeton made the observation that for leavening cakes: 'As eggs are used instead of yeast, they should always be very thoroughly whisked.' Yeast-raised cakes may have lost popularity because they did not keep as well as egg-raised cakes. By the late 19th century baking powder had replaced yeast entirely as a leavener for cakes.

The hallowed formula of fruit cake with marzipan on top and icing on top of that was first put into print by Mrs Raffald in 1782 and has held its place until now. Fruit cakes, rich or plain depending on the means of the household, were regarded with great affection by the British middle classes for most of the 20th century. They went into the tuck boxes of children at boarding schools, and were much used for picnics and shooting parties. Most people regarded them as robust, nutritious, comforting food. This was a complete change in attitude from that displayed by Eliza Acton in *Modern Cookery for Private Families*, who said that 'more illness is caused by habitual indulgence in the richer and heavier kinds of cakes than could easily be credited by persons who have given no attention to the subject'.

Gingerbread: a product which is always spiced, and normally with ginger, but which varies considerably in shape and texture. Some modern British gingerbreads are so crisp that they might qualify to be called ginger biscuits. Others are definitely cake-like.

In the recent past many British towns had their gingerbread specialities whose recipes are still known.

Examples are Ashbourne (a 'white' gingerbread) and Ormskirk (a 'dark' one). Some Scottish gingerbreads resemble shortbread, e.g. the Edinburgh speciality which was known as parliament cake (or 'parlies') in the 19th century. A thin crisp gingerbread, it is made with treacle and brown sugar, cut into squares after baking; it is thought to be so called because it was eaten by the members of the Scottish Parliament.

Grasmere gingerbread, from the Lake District, also has a shortbread texture. Originally it was based on oatmeal, as were broonie, an Orkney gingerbread recorded by F. Marian McNeill, and parkin.

Late medieval gingerbread in England had been made from a thick mixture of honey and breadcrumbs, sometimes coloured with saffron or sanders (powdered sandalwood). Cinnamon and pepper were added for flavour. Made into a square, the confection was decorated with box leaves nailed down with gilded cloves.

Gingerbread was also ornamented by impressing designs within wooden moulds. The moulds were sometimes very large and elaborate and beautifully carved. In England, such confections were bought at fairs and, together with other sweet treats, were known under the collective name of 'fairings'. The habit of shaping gingerbread figures of men and pigs, especially for Bonfire Night (5 November), survives in Britain.

In the 17th century white gingerbread became fashionable. This was an almond paste confection resembling spiced marzipan. Its surface was ornamented with real or imitation gold leaf, from which comes the expression 'gilt on the gingerbread'.

Generally, during the 16th and 17th centuries, ginger-bread became lighter; breadcrumbs were replaced by flour. Treacle was used instead of honey from the mid-17th century on. Butter and eggs became popular additions, enriching the mixture; and raising agents were added to lighten it further.

Gooseberry: the fruit of bushes of several species of the genus *Ribes*, of which *R. grossularia*, the European gooseberry, is the principal cultivated species. Goose-berry bushes grow wild in most of the northern temperate zone, flourishing in cool, moist, or high regions where many other fruiting plants do not thrive.

Most wild species are thorny. The berries are 12 mm (0.5") or more in diameter, dark or pale green (the latter often called 'white'), yellow, or red, with firm skins which may be either hairy or smooth. The flavour is often sour.

Gooseberries were late to be taken into cultivation. The earliest record is said to be a fruiterer's bill from the court of the English King Edward I, dated 1276, for gooseberry bushes imported from France. However, the fruit has never been widely popular in France. It is traditionally used in northern parts of the country to make a sauce for fish, which explains its French name *groseille maquereau* (mackerel currant). As for the English name, Johnson (1847) has a theory:

Dr Martyun considers the name was applied to this fruit, in consequence of its being employed as sauce for that bird. It is somewhat unfortunate for this derivation that it has never been so used. It seems to me most probably to be a corruption of the Dutch name Kruisbes, or Gruisbes, derived from Kruis, the Cross, and Bes, as Berry, because the fruit was ready for use just after the Festival of the Invention of the Holy Cross; just as Kruis-haring, in Dutch, is a herring, caught after the same festival.

The *OED*, however, adheres to the derivation from goose, in favour of which it may be said that the sharpness of the gooseberry goes well with a fatty or oily meat (e.g. goose or mackerel). Dallas in *Kettner's Book of the Table* observes that the older herbalists always insisted that gooseberry was so called because it was used as a sauce for goose. He concedes, however, that there could be an alternative derivation linked with the Scottish name for the berry, groset or grosart, and continues:

The Scotch, it must be remembered are great in gooseberries. It is a northern fruit. When there was not a tree nor a shrub to be found in the Shetland islands and the Orkneys, there were goosberry bushes in abundance; and it was an old joke against the Shetlanders, that when they read their Bibles and tried to picture to themselves Adam hiding among the trees of the garden, they could only call up in vision a naked man cowering under a grosart bush. The gooseberries of Scotland are the perfection of their race, and for flavour and variety far beyond those of the south – just as English gooseberries are better than those of the Continent. On the Continent they are little prized, and not very well known. The French have no name for them, distinct from that of red currants.

It was in England that the popularity of the gooseberry led to improved, larger and sweeter varieties being bred. A distinction was made between dessert gooseberries, for eating raw, and cooking gooseberries, which are sour but have a superior flavour when cooked. From the late 18th century and throughout the 19th amateur 'gooseberry clubs' were set up in the Midlands and the north of England. These held competitions for the best-flavoured and, more particularly, for the largest fruit. Johnson points out that extraordinary results were achieved, especially in the vicinity of Manchester, by 'the lowest and most illiterate members of society, [who] by continual experience and perseverance in growing and raising new sorts, have brought the fruit to weigh three times as much as before and that, too, under the greatest disadvantages, not having the privilege of soil, manure, situation, &c. like the gardeners of their more wealthy neighbours'.

A few similar clubs existed in N. America. In England, in the 1980s, fewer than 10 such clubs survived, mostly in Cheshire. But the best known is the Egton Bridge Old Gooseberry Society, in Yorkshire. This was founded around 1800, and has held annual competitions (except for one or two years in the First World War) ever since. The sole criterion is weight. A new Egton Bridge record was established in 1985 when the champion berry, of the yellow variety Woodpecker, weighed 30 drams 22 grains (1.925 oz); but the world record (58 g/ 2.06 oz) was still held at that time by a Woodpecker shown at Marton in Cheshire in 1978. Giant gooseberries are produced by removing all the growing berries but one from a plant.

In 1905 a mildew disease was accidentally introduced from America, wiping out the whole crop of European gooseberries. The plant was re-established by crossing with American species resistant to mildew, but the gooseberry has never fully regained its earlier popularity.

'Gooseberry' is a long-standing British slang term for an unwanted third person at a lovers' meeting; and of disparagement generally. But a good, ripe gooseberry can stand comparison with most other soft fruits. Gooseberry fool a frothy purée with whipped cream, and gooseberry tansy, a rich, firm dessert with eggs and butter, are renowned.

The eating quality of gooseberries cannot be predicted from their colour or hairiness. Some thornless varieties of the plant have been developed, for ease of picking.

Hasty pudding: the simplest of all puddings, if it can be called a pudding at all, for it is no more than a porridge of flour and milk. Such a pudding could be made in little more time than it took to boil the milk, and it has no doubt been a popular emergency dish since the Middle Ages, if not earlier. Sweetened, flavoured with spice or rosewater, and dotted with butter, hasty pudding can be quite palatable; and in fact in the 18th and 19th centuries in England it was esteemed as a delicacy. Before 1800, an egg was often added to the mixture, though after this time mixtures with egg were given other names.

A hasty pudding hybrid is Malvern pudding, made of alternate layers of hasty pudding with egg and of sweetened cooked apple; it is baked.

In the far north of England, and in Scotland, at least as early as the 18th century, the name came to be applied to a plain porridge of oats and barley, made with water as often as milk. In Victorian England, too, hasty pudding was sometimes made with oatmeal, or with sago or with tapioca. Milk was always used. This pudding evolved into what are called 'nursery milk puddings' in Britain; the name 'hasty pudding' is no longer used, but it is agreeable to reread what May Byron had to say about it while it still bore its old name:

There are certain traditional puddings which have never lost their high repute. Of such is the celebrated hasty pudding with which Jack the Giant-killer filled, not his mouth, but the bag beneath his doublet. 'Ods bobs!' cried his Welsh antagonist, 'hur can do that hurself,' and, unwarily swallowing an immense bowlful of the dainty, he was rent as by some high-explosive. Now, hasty pudding is the very meekest and mildest of all its tribe: butter (literally) won't melt in its mouth, unless it be scalding hot out of the saucepan. It is a tame, colourless, flavourless affair *per se*; yet, look you (as the Giant would have said), it has proudly survived, on this one noble achievement, the wear and tear of centuries. Still puddings run deep.

High tea: is a substantial late afternoon or early evening meal. The term has been in use since the mid-19th century and distinguishes it from the lighter, more elegant afternoon tea; and yet, to those who take either, they are simply tea. This is shown in the way Arnold Bennett manipulates the word in this quotation from *Anna of the Five Towns*, a novel set in the Potteries district of Staffordshire:

The tea, made specially magnificent in honour of the betrothal, was such a meal as could only have been compassed in Staffordshire or Yorkshire – a high tea of the last richness and excellence, exquisitely gracious to the palate, but ruthless in its demands on the stomach. At one end of the table, which glittered with silver, glass, and Longshaw china, was a fowl which had been boiled for four hours; at the other, a hot pork pie, islanded in liquor, which might have satisfied a regiment. Between these two dishes were all the delicacies which differentiate high tea from tea, and on the quality of which the success of the meal really depends; hot pikelets, hot crumpets, hot toast, sardines with tomatoes, raisin bread, currant bread, seed-cake, lettuce, home-made marmalade, and home-made hams. The repast occupied over an hour, and even then not a quarter of the food was consumed.

'Teas' similar to the one described above crop up over and over again in English fiction and diaries from the mid 19th to the early 20th centuries; the constants are abundance and variety of food, the presence of ham or pie, salad, the choice of baked goods, preserves, and a fine display of table ware. Tea also became strongly linked in popular culture with abundant Yorkshire hospitality. Brears gives an account of a substantial Yorkshire tea which actually took place. It was held by Miss Maffin in her small Wharfedale cottage about the 1860s. The round cricket table in the centre of the room, although barely a yard across, had been laid with her best china, a seed cake, bread and butter, ham sandwiches, and a salad of lettuce, cress, radishes and onions. Tea cakes regularly replaced the lid of the kettle, to become hot and moist in its steam, while muffins were toasted on a toasting-dog before the fire.

When her friends arrived, they arranged themselves around the table. It was *de rigueur* on state occasions like this for the ladies to sit fair and square to the table in the ordinary manner; but the gentlemen were allowed more latitude. Indeed, among the older generation, the correct claim to dignity seems to have been to sit with your chair sideways to the table, and your back to your hostess, your bread and salad or your ham sandwiches on your red spotted handkerchief spread across your knees, and your cup and saucer on the edge of the table. Seated in this manner, the company then proceeded to do full justice to the fare set out before them, the conversation flowing just as freely as the hot tea laced with rum.

The eating of tea, and the existence of two forms, afternoon tea and high tea, provides a lesson in British social history. Habitual consumption of either (it is not the custom to take both in any given day) says much about an individual's background and daily life. Afternoon tea, eaten after a light lunch and before a larger mid-evening dinner, is considered an indicator of a leisured, comfortable existence. High tea, eaten on arrival home from work, is popularly associated with old-fashioned households, rural or urban working-class backgrounds; although not invariably so, as Michael Smith points out, quoting from an unnamed earlier author:

High Tea. In some houses this is a permanent institution, quite taking the place of late dinner, and to many it is a most enjoyable meal, young people preferring it to dinner, it being a movable feast that can be partaken of at hours which will not interfere with tennis, boating or other amusements.

At high tea, the means and desires of the household and demands of the occasion dictate exactly what goes on the table. Cold cuts, meat pies, salads, pickles, crumpets, muffins, teacakes, preserves, honey, fruit loaves, cakes and sponges are all considered suitable foods, participants selecting according to tastes and appetite. Tea (Indian) is drunk throughout the meal, although coffee or cocoa may be served if preferred.

The origins of high tea are uncertain, but evidence indicates they are different from those of afternoon tea, and that meals of the high tea type were well established by the mid-19th century. 'High' seems to have been added to the name by people less familiar with it – those from a wealthy urban background, who adopted it as a novelty, or because it was conveniently timed for children, or as a cheaper, less formal alternative to dinner – from which the meal may actually have descended.

Kendal mint cake: a confection of hard crystalline sugar heavily flavoured with mint and shaped into slabs, has been made in Kendal in the English Lake District since at least the mid-19th century. It is promoted as an energy-giving food for polar explorers and mountaineers.

Kipper: now usually a noun but formerly also a verb, meaning a method of curing herring (formerly also salmon) by splitting open, salting, and smoking.

The kipper is a British institution and is perceived as part of what a gastronomic writer of the French sort would call 'Britain's culinary heritage'. However, in its present form, as applied to herring, it only dates back to the first half of the 19th century. It was in the 1840s that a Northumbrian curer, after years of experiment, launched his kippered herring on the London market. He borrowed his term from a cure applied to salmon, but how far that went back is not clear. (References to 'kippered salmon' are known from as early as the 15th century, but there is room for doubt in interpreting them since 'kipper' was a term for a spent salmon, i.e. one which had done its spawning and survived in poor, emaciated condition. It may be, as Cutting suggests, that such salmon were made more readily saleable by the kippering process, and that this was how the process got its name.)

The best kippers are produced on an artisanal basis in Scotland, the Isle of Man, and a few places (such as Craster in Northumberland) in England. Those made on a larger scale may be quite acceptable, but suffer by comparison with the best and will have been treated with an artificial dye (permitted but undesirable).

Kippers are easily cooked, by frying or grilling (US broiling) or 'jugging'.

A stir was caused in the 1990s by the publication of a French official work which seemed to suggest, while acknowledging the existence of British kippers, that a similar product made in the north of France was the original or dominant version; but the suggestion disappeared from the next printing. The incident does, however, point to the need to acknowledge here that there is such a thing as a French kipper.

Lardy cake: a traditional English tea bread popular in country areas. It is made from bread dough enriched with lard and sugar and, usually, spices and dried fruit. The dough is rolled and folded several times to give a layered texture.

Lardy cakes were originally intended as special celebration cakes, made only at harvest time or for family festivals. Elizabeth David remarks that 'It was only when sugar became cheap, and when the English taste for sweet things – particularly in the Midlands and the North – became more pronounced, that such rich breads or cakes were made or could be bought from the bakery every week.'

In the days when ovens were fired only once a week, and in some households only once a fortnight, for the baking of a very large batch of bread and dough products, any dough not used for making the daily bread was transformed into richer products such as lardy cakes, which thus earned the alternative name 'scrap cakes'.

They might also be called 'flead cakes' – flead is a light kind of lard scraped off a pig's internal membranes. The high fat content in such cakes would prevent them drying out as much as ordinary bread.

Lobscouse: the English name for a dish, or rather group of dishes, which almost certainly has its origin in the Baltic ports, especially those of Germany. In all its forms, the name refers to a seaman's dish; and in England it is particularly associated, in recent times, with the port of Liverpool, which is why Liverpudlians are often referred to as 'scouses' or 'scousers'. The dish has, however, a long history in other nearby parts of England. Thus Hone (1826) relates that at what were called 'Merrynights' in N. Lancashire and Cumberland and Westmorland, lobscouse was served after the dancing.

As with many similar dishes, there are numerous and fiercely disputed variations. However, the following account may be taken as typical. Lobscouse is made in a single pot and begins by frying or 'sweating' in dripping, sliced onions, carrots, and turnips. Stewing steak or mutton or corned beef is added; plus, when the meat is browned, salt, pepper, and water. Sometimes a cow-heel or pig's trotter is put in to give a gelatinous body to the dish. Chopped potatoes are always included. At this stage it can be put in the oven to cook for a long time.

Some insist that ship's biscuit should be crumbled into the dish, while others maintain that pearl barley is an essential ingredient.

A Liverpool street chant parodies 'The Charge of the Light Brigade':

Half a Leg, Half a Leg, Half a Leg of Mutton,
Into the Pan of Scouse rolled the six onions.

Labskaus, the German version, may be made with either fish (*Fischlabskaus*) or meat; in either case, preserved rather than fresh.

In Denmark the dish, traditionally made with salt beef, is known as *skipperlabskovs* and is supposed to be thick enough to eat with a fork but not so thick that the fork can stand up in it. (Some Liverpudlians agree and say that it should be firm enough for a mouse to be able to trot over it but mushy and capable of being spread on bread to make a 'lobby butty'.)

This subject and other kindred ones have been brilliantly and entertainingly illuminated by Anne Grossman and Lisa Thomas in a work providing a gastronomic companion to the famous naval novels of Patrick O'Brian.

Maids of honour: are pastry tartlets filled with a white curd which is usually made with renneted milk and cream, butter, sugar, almonds, eggs, and lemon juice and zest. They have a historical association with Richmond and Kew in Surrey.

Various stories associate them with Tudor royalty but no one has been able to establish whether the maids of honour were themselves the main consumers or simply used them to please royal palates. The first reference in print is 1769 in the *Public Advertiser*.

Mince pie: in Britain, is a miniature round pie, filled with mincemeat: typically a mixture of dried fruits, chopped nuts and apples, suet, spices, and lemon juice, vinegar, or brandy. Although the filling is called mincemeat, it rarely contains meat nowadays.

In N. America the pie may be larger, to serve several people. The large size is an innovation, for the original forms were almost always small. The earliest type was a small medieval pastry called a chewette, which contained chopped meat or liver, or fish on fast days, mixed with chopped hard-boiled egg and ginger. This might be baked or fried. It became usual to enrich the filling with dried fruit and other sweet ingredients.

Already by the 16th century 'minced' or 'shred' pies, as they were then known, had become a Christmas speciality, which they still are. The beef was sometimes partly or wholly replaced by suet from the mid-17th century onwards, and meat had effectively disappeared from 'mincemeat' on both sides of the Atlantic in the 19th century.

Mildred P. Blakelock (*c.*1932) wrote entertainingly of customs and superstitions associated with mince pies. She asked:

Is it lucky to eat as many as possible before Christmas, as says the dweller in London, or is the more elaborate custom found in Yorkshire more correct? The writer of this book, being a

Yorkshire woman, is quite sure that it is not correct to eat mince pies before Christmas, but to eat one in a different house if possible on each of the twelve days of the season of Christmas. Anyone who does this ensures a happy year, as each mince pie so eaten is supposed to bring a happy month!

Muffin: a term connected with *moufflet*, an old French word applied to bread, meaning 'soft'.

The English muffin is round and made from a soft yeast-leavened dough enriched with milk and butter. It is usually cooked on a griddle, which gives it a flat, golden-brown top and bottom, with a white band around the waist and a light, spongy interior. For serving, muffins are toasted back and front and then split with the fingers by easing them apart at the joint all the way round. Some butter is placed inside, and the two halves put back together and kept warm. This method appears as early as 1747 and was recommended by Hannah Glasse, who said that the inside of muffins should be like honeycomb. Writers on the subject of muffins agree that they should not be cut with a knife, as this makes them heavy.

Muffins were most popular during the 19th century, when muffin men traversed town streets at teatime, ringing their bells. In the 1840s the muffin-man's bell was prohibited by Act of Parliament because many people objected to it, but the prohibition was ineffective. In recent times, muffins have regained some popularity; in common with crumpets and pikelets, they provide a physical base and a pretext for eating melted butter.

The word 'muffin' first appeared in print in the early

18th century, and recipes began to be published in the middle of the 18th century. There has always been some confusion between muffins, crumpets, and pikelets, both in recipes and in name. 'Muffin' usually meant a breadlike product (sometimes simply made from whatever bread dough was available), as opposed to the more pancake-like crumpets.

Mutton: is the meat of domestic sheep over one year old. It has a stronger flavour and deeper colour than lamb. Formerly it was much liked and eaten in Britain; Mrs Beeton commented that it was 'undoubtedly the meat most generally used in families'. It was taken from animals between three and five years old, among which wethers (castrated males) were considered to yield the best meat.

Mutton production has, however, dwindled during the 20th century, as sheep were bred to grow and fatten quickly. Now it is a rarity.

A mutton carcass is larger than that of a lamb, but the pattern of jointing is the same. Mutton should be aged for longer than lamb; two to three weeks were common in the past.

Because mutton is now largely a thing of the past in Britain, recipes for it have either transferred themselves to lamb, or become items of historical interest. Plain spit-roasting or boiling were, no doubt, methods used from early times; but what one finds in early English cookery books are complex and highly flavoured mutton recipes. Thus, Sir Hugh Platt (1609) gave a recipe 'To boyle a Legge of Mutton in the French fashion', which required the cook to hollow the meat out of the leg, chop it with beef suet and marrow, and work it into a mixture of cream, egg yolks, raisins, dates, and bread, stuff the mixture back in, and boil the joint. Similar recipes, becoming steadily simpler, reappeared over the next two centuries, eventually transforming into Mrs Beeton's stuffed leg of mutton, in which the bone was replaced by a plain forcemeat and the joint roasted.

Sharp ingredients, such as verjuice vinegar, and lemon, were frequently called for in sauces and gravies for mutton during the 17th century. Carbonadoes, thin slices of mutton cross-hatched with knife cuts, were grilled and served with onions and vinegar, or cooked with white wine and lemon. Many mutton dishes were spiced with cloves, cinnamon, and nutmeg, and cooked with aromatic herbs and lemon or orange peel. Sugar appears in some recipes, notably pies.

In the 18th century, the spices, apart from mace, nutmeg, and pepper, largely disappeared, as did the sourer ingredients. Oysters, anchovies, and mushrooms took their place, being put into the gravy or served under the meat as a 'ragoo'. Sliced lemons were a common garnish, and barberries enjoyed a vogue during the early 18th century. Cucumbers, cooked in sauce or gravy, were also popular with mutton. Capers (or pickled nasturtium seeds) were intermittently used from the 17th century onwards, and by the mid-19th century had become the accepted accompaniment for boiled leg of mutton. Redcurrant jelly was served with mutton from the late 18th century onwards.

Harico (from the French *haricot*, stew) came to England during the 17th century, a stew of mutton, turnips, and carrots; it remained a dish of English home cookery well into the 20th. In the 17th and 18th centuries, hashes of mutton were made from partially roasted joints cut in thin slices, and heated with gravy and seasonings. By the 19th century this had become a method for using up cold mutton, by reheating it in gravy with onions. One elaborate version of a hash was given by Charles Carter (1730) as 'Shoulder of Mutton disguis'd'; it involved cutting all the meat off a shoulder without piercing the skin, cooking the meat with seasonings, and then placing the blade bone in the middle of the mixture and covering it over with the skin. This curious recipe resurfaced from time to time, notably as Mrs Raffald's 'Hen and Chickens', and made a late and surprising appearance in Mrs Beeton as 'Hashed Lamb and Broiled Blade Bone'.

Mutton (or lamb) was a popular pie filling from the 17th century until the 19th century. Two distinct types of pie seem to have existed. First, there were sweet mutton or lamb pies, whose history probably stretches back much further into medieval cookery. These involved raisins, dates, sugar, candied peel, cinnamon, and cloves, as well as the meat, and must have been well liked, for they appear in recipe books well into the 18th century, long after sugar had vanished from other meat dishes. Secondly, savoury mutton pies, usually filled with cutlets and forcemeat, or with caudles of eggs, or ragoos (ragout) of oysters added after cooking, were also made. These continued to find favour well into the

19th century. Scottish mutton pies were apparently well liked by Dr Johnson, although it is not obvious whether they were sweet or savoury. More recent Scottish recipes for little hot mutton pies call for seasonings of salt, pepper, and mace or nutmeg, and a crust made with beef suet by a hot-water method; such pies remain very popular.

In the hilly sheep-farming districts of Britain, a boiled mutton pudding, encased in suet crust and very similar to the better-known (beef) steak and kidney pudding, used to be made. It included sheep's kidney, onion, and flour. Other additions were rowan-berries in season, or pickled damsons, or pickled capers.

Mutton was sometimes used to mimic venison, and there were also recipes for converting it to 'hams'. 'Braxty' mutton was meat from a sheep which had died from natural causes or met with an accident. Not everyone was willing to eat this.

Using up the remains of joints has for long been a preoccupation for British cooks (witness books with titles like '50 Ways of Using up Cold Mutton'). This version of 'Vicarage Mutton' was quoted by Dorothy Hartley; 'Hot on Sunday, Cold on Monday, Hashed on Tuesday, Minced on Wednesday, Curried on Thursday, Broth on Friday, Cottage pie Saturday.' This, when it first appeared under the now familiar name in the latter part of the 19th century, was a mutton dish. Mutton also appeared in Irish stew and Lancashire hotpot, and in other dishes on British tables up until the Second World War, although it became less and less common, and was finally replaced by the meat now referred to as 'lamb'.

Parson's nose: has been described with her usual lucidity by Theodora FitzGibbon:

a colloquial English expression for the small fatty joint which holds the tail feathers of poultry. When well crisped after roasting, it is considered a tasty morsel by some people. When the bird concerned is a cooked goose or duck rather than a turkey or a chicken, the joint is called 'the pope's nose,' although, in a general way, Protestant communities are said to use the latter expression and Catholic communities the former!

The French term *sot-l'y-laisse*, meaning 'only a fool would leave it', refers to a morsel of meat positioned just above the parson's nose and also considered to be a delicacy.

Pasty: nowadays a medium-sized or small pastry turnover, seldom larger than an individual serving.

The word pasty came into English, via old French, from the Latin *pasta* (dough). In the Middle Ages, pasties were often very large, and generally meant meat or fish, well seasoned, enclosed in pastry and baked (similar to modern *en croûte* dishes). While pasties were made without a mould and contained a single type of filling, a pie contained a mixture and eventually became the name for the deeper, raised form. In both, the pastry was made to recipes and baked in a way that would make it too tough to be eaten.

Medieval pasties often contained joints of meat or

whole birds; C. Anne Wilson quotes an ordinance of Richard II in 1378 for prices charged by cooks and pie bakers, including those for capons and hens baked in pasties. Beef, mutton, and game were also used; porpoise meat, which counted as fish, was made into pasties for fast days. Venison pasty was popular for many centuries, and was probably a status symbol, as beef was sometimes marinated in supposed imitation, a practice which appears to have gone on into the 17th century. Butter or beef marrow were often added to pasties generally, to help keep the meat moist.

Smaller, sweet pasties were also made; one medieval type was petyperneux (or pernollys), possibly meaning 'little lost eggs'. Containing whole egg yolks, currants and raisins, bone marrow, and spices in paste made of fine flour with saffron, sugar, and salt, these were fried. Later forms included the 'hat' (with the addition of pounded meat or fish), and, by the 16th century, a turnover shape known as a peascod (pea pod), whose filling included chopped kidney. Moulds in that shape, or in the form of a dolphin, were evidently used for making these. Large pasties were decorated with elaborate patterns cut out of rolled pastry.

The best-known pasty of modern times is the Cornish pasty, made in a pointed oval shape, with a seam of crimped pastry running the full length of the upper side. In the recent past, fillings varied. Cubed beef with root vegetables is now considered standard, but other meats or fish, or vegetables alone, were used. Theodora FitzGibbon recounts, 'It is said in Cornwall that the Devil never crossed the River Tamar into that county for fear of the Cornish woman's habit of putting anything and everything into a pasty.' The corners of the pasties could be marked with initials to identify the recipient. Sometimes very large pasties for a whole family were made. Some pasties contained two courses, so to speak; a savoury filling at one end and a sweet one at the other. Sometimes a very large family-size pasty would be made and taken to the local baker's shop to be baked.

Dorothy Hartley described a foot, a pasty traditionally eaten in Lancashire. The name comes from the form of the pasty crust. A piece of shortcrust pastry is rolled into an oval shape, then one end is rolled much thinner, so that it spreads out and the pastry assumes the form of the sole and heel of a shoe. Filling is put on the thick end, and the thin part wrapped over it and pressed down around the edge.

Something akin to the Cornish pasty is made in the county of Somerset; this is a priddy oggy (oggy is Cornish dialect for pasty) which appears to have been invented in the late 1960s. It is filled with pork, and the pastry contains cheese.

Other types of pasty include the Bedfordshire clanger (with suet crust enclosing a meat filling at one end and a sweet filling at the other), and the Yorkshire mint pasty, a large one with a sweet filling of raisins, currants, candied peel, brown sugar, and butter, liberally flavoured with fresh mint and lightly spiced.

Pease pudding: (alternatively known as pease porridge) is a peculiarly British dish, on account of the long-standing preference in Britain for peas over other pulses. It began its career in remote antiquity as pease pottage, a thick porridge made from the dried mealy peas that were a staple food; this was the most usual way of preparing them. Pease pottage and, when available, bacon went together in the diet of simple country people. The bacon was heavily salted and the pease pottage, made without salt, balanced the flavour.

At the beginning of the 17th century the introduction of the pudding cloth allowed pease pudding, a more solid product, to be made. Usually the ingredients consisted only of peas (previously soaked, if dried peas are used), and a little flavouring: sugar and pepper, and sometimes mint, were commonly used. The ingredients were mixed and simply cooked in a pudding cloth in simmering liquid, perhaps alongside a piece of bacon, for which the pudding would be a fine accompaniment. Sometimes this very solid pudding was lightened with breadcrumbs, or a little egg or butter were used to enrich it. Pease pudding has now lost its importance in the British diet, but remains popular in the north. One can even buy it in cans.

It has been suggested that the old nursery rhyme:

> Pease pudding hot,
> Pease pudding cold,
> Pease pudding in the pot
> Nine days old

referred not to the inevitable appearance of the dish at all meals but to the making of a fermented product like a semi-solid version of Indonesian tempe, or a primitive form of Japanese miso. Certainly, if the procedure in the rhyme were followed, boiling, cooling, and leaving for nine days, micro-organisms naturally present would have caused some kind of fermentation to take place, but unless some kind of starter had been used, the most likely result would have been spoilage.

Pork pie: The British pork pie and its relative, the veal and ham pie, are survivals of the medieval tradition of raised pies, and have changed surprisingly little. This particular pie, simply known as 'pork pie', is of a form distinct from other pies which merely happen to be made with pork. The filling is of fresh pork without other major ingredients, seasoned with salt, pepper, and a small quantity of herbs, especially sage.

At Melton Mowbray in Leicestershire, long famous for its pork pies, anchovy essence was added not only for its flavour but because it was thought to give the meat an attractive pink colour, while pies from other districts were brownish or greyish. In modern pies, which are always pink, the colour is achieved by the use of chemicals.

The case is made from a hot water paste of flour, lard, and boiling salted water, well kneaded to give it strength. A small hole is left in the centre of the lid. Traditionally there was a decorative rosette around the hole. Sometimes hinged metal corsets are used to stop the case of the pie from sagging during baking.

Present-day pies are almost always supported, so that

they have sheer vertical sides, whereas those of former times used to bulge slightly. The support is removed towards the end of the baking to allow the pastry to brown. Once the pie is baked, and while still hot, rich stock made from trimmings is poured in through the hole by means of a funnel. When the pie cools the stock sets into a protective jelly.

Pork pies are circular when small or medium sized, and are also made as long, rectangular 'gala pies' – for a gala or miners' festival. Large pies used to contain eggs and sometimes also pickled walnuts; but now eggs are more usual in veal and ham pies, and walnuts are never used.

Portable soup: a product which achieved some prominence in 18th-century English cookery books, was a precursor (and a relatively sophisticated and refined one) of 19th-century meat extracts and 20th-century stock cubes. Bradley (1736) explained in his agreeable prose the benefits of the product, describing it as:

[a] curious Preparation for the use of Gentlemen that travel; the use of which I esteem to be of extraordinary Service to such as travel in wild and open Countries, where few or no Provisions are to be met with; and it will be of no less Benefit to such Families as have not immediate Recourse to Markets, for the Readiness of it for making of Soups, or its Use where Gravey is required; and particularly to those that travel, the lightness of its Carriage, the small room it takes up, and the easy way of putting it in use, renders it extremely serviceable. This is what one may call Veal-Glue.

It was made by taking a lot of meat and boiling it lengthily then reducing the liquid to a syrupy consistency, after which it would dry quite hard and keep well until the time came to reconstitute it with boiling water. Aromatics or other flavourings could be used in boiling the meat or added at the reconstitution stage.

Hannah Glasse gave two recipes, one lifted from an earlier work (as was her wont). Both state that a piece of the 'Glew' the size of a walnut is enough for a pint of water. The second recipe, listing the various dishes and ways in which it can be used, could be translated without great difficulty into 'tips on use' to be printed on a modern stock cube or 'instant soup' packet.

Portable soup in its original form survived, at least in recipe books, into the 19th century. How many travellers actually carried it around in their pockets or in little tin boxes, as recommended, is a question which seems unlikely ever to receive a satisfactory answer.

Posset: in its earliest medieval form was a drink made from milk lightly curdled by adding an acid liquid such as wine, ale, citrus juice, to it. It was sweetened and often spiced. Sometimes the curds and whey were separated and the curds mixed with conventional junket curds, breadcrumbs, and honey to make an 'eating posset' that was thick enough to slice. In the 17th century sack (like sweet sherry), claret, or orange juice were used in eating possets. There were rich versions containing cream and eggs. Later additions in the 18th century included almonds and crumbled Naples biscuits (sponge fingers) and brandy might be added to the wine. By now the dish had more or less lost its identity, and soon lost its name; it developed into the early types of trifle and into various 'creams', which contained fewer eggs or none and resembled a syllabub or a fruit fool.

Sack posset, long the most popular type, became first 'sack cream' and then, when it was made with white wine in the 19th century and the reason for the name was forgotten, 'suck cream'.

Quaking pudding: is a pudding with a light, frail texture which is halfway to being an egg custard. Most of what solidity it has comes from breadcrumbs. This is one of the oldest of the puddings made in a cloth. A recipe for it was recorded early in the 17th century, and it also appears in Samuel Pepys's diary; he recalls having eaten a particularly good 'shaking pudding'. This pudding is often served with a sweet white wine sauce.

Roast: Roasting meat was something at which the British were, indeed are, supposed to excel. An 18th-century visitor to England from Sweden, Per Kalm, remarked that 'the English men understand almost better than any other people the art of properly roasting a joint'. Admittedly, he qualified the compliment by observing that the English art of cooking did not extend much beyond roast beef and plum pudding, but still it was a compliment; and the French term *rosbifs* for

Englishmen may also be taken as including at least a touch of affection, although usually derogatory.

Rock: a British sweet made in large and colourful sticks. There are two types: ordinary rock, sold at seaside resorts and other places visited by tourists, and Edinburgh rock, which is the original form of the sweet but remains mainly a local speciality of Edinburgh. Ordinary rock is a sweet of the plain pulled candy type, which is always professionally made, since it demands very complex pulling techniques. Each cylindrical stick consists of a coloured outer layer enclosing a white core with lettering made of coloured candy ('A present from Llandudno' or something of the kind) which runs the whole length of the stick, so that each letter is actually a long strip whose cross-section is that of the letter, and wherever the rock is broken the exposed ends will show a legible inscription (though one of them will show the letters in reverse. The letters are made in a fairly large size from hot coloured sugar and surrounded by a white matrix and coloured outer layer; then the assembly is drawn out to great length so that it becomes quite narrow. Sometimes the sticks are as long and thick as a child's arm.

Although the history of pulled sugar and pulled candy goes back to the Middle Ages, rock with letters in it is probably a recent invention. The first person who remarked on it was Henry Mayhew in the 1860s, in his study of the work of Londoners, where he noted that a sweet vendor had recently introduced short sentences into sugar sticks. Examples included 'Do you love me',

'Do you love sprats', and 'Sir Robert Peel' – the last remembering a then recently dead Prime Minister.

Edinburgh rock comes in much smaller sticks, pastel coloured and with a peculiar chalky consistency. It is made from a conventional sugar syrup in which little attempt is made to inhibit crystallization, so that during pulling a mass of very small crystals is formed. It is left exposed to the air for a day after making, during which it absorbs moisture and becomes quite crumbly. White Edinburgh rock is flavoured with vanilla, lemon, or mint; pink with raspberry or rose water; yellow with orange; and beige with ginger. Although the vast majority of Edinburgh rock is made professionally (still mainly in Edinburgh), it can be made at home.

Rock cake: (sometimes rock bun, as in some late 19th-century references cited by the *OED*), a fairly plain and solid small cake/bun, usually enlivened with raisins (or currants) and candied peel. Rock cakes take their name from their irregular craggy appearance, not from their consistency. They are made by baking uneven lumps of dryish dough on baking sheets.

Recipes dating back to the 1860s are recorded; a range of flavourings including mace, lemon zest, and brandy were used in early examples. Arnold Palmer has a reference to City gentlemen in London in the 1870s standing at a counter and lunching 'off a glass of sherry with a rock cake or a couple of biscuits'. The use of currants, which became standard in the 20th century, is attested from the 1880s.

Roly-poly pudding: a widely used name for a suet pudding made in a roll shape. The name is generally given to a pudding with a sweet filling such as jam, or treacle and breadcrumbs, or mixed dried fruits with marmalade; in each case spread over the flat sheet of dough and rolled up. However, there are also savoury types, for example, bacon pudding which was often made in this shape.

The lasting fame of the name was conferred by Beatrix Potter's quietly horrifying book *The Tale of Samuel Whiskers or The Roly Poly Pudding* in which the stuffing of the pudding was a savoury one. The hero, Tom Kitten, was to be the stuffing, but fortunately he escaped.

Formerly roly-poly pudding was boiled in a pudding cloth; but the skill of enclosing a pudding of this shape in a cloth has now mostly been lost. Since it could not be adapted to a basin as could a round pudding, it is now almost invariably baked. However, the change of technique has been applauded by no less an authority than May Byron, who also notes an interesting gender-related point about it:

Roly-poly pudding, however (also euphoniously known as dog-in-a-basket), appeals to the masculine appetite as nothing else can do. If you doubt this assertion, go into a City restaurant at midday, and scrutinise the customers' faces when they hear that 'jam roll is off.' It does not need to be accompanied by the gammon and spinach of the nursery rhyme. It is indeed sufficient unto itself. And when it is baked instead of boiled . . . then, as Humpty Dumpty said, 'there's glory for you!'

Sandwich: a term, and indeed an object, whose origin is generally attributed to John Montagu, the 4th Earl of Sandwich, who according to the *NSOED* is 'said to have eaten food in this form so as to avoid having to leave the gaming table'. Ayto cites a work of 1770, *Londres*, by the author Grosley in support of this view, and remarks that the first use of the word in print occurs in the journal of Edward Gibbon for 24 November 1762, when he had dinner at an establishment which he regarded as 'truly English' and was able to observe numerous important contemporaries supping off cold meat 'or a Sandwich'.

Butties and sarnies are English slang terms for sandwiches, the former north country and long established, the latter more recent. In terms of gentility a Liverpool chip butty is at the opposite end of the spectrum from the decorous and delicate little cucumber sandwiches which appear on British afternoon tea tables.

Fernie (1905) had a remarkable knack for picking up amusing and arresting anecdotes or quotations to enliven what he wrote about foods. Here are three examples from his entry on Sandwich.

- [From *The Pickwick Papers*] 'What are all them clerks eating Sandvidges for?' asked Mr Weller, senior, of his son, Sam, when they went together to the Will Office, at the Bank of England. 'Cos it's their dooty, I suppose,' replied Sam; 'it's a part o' the system: they're allvays a-doin' it here, all day long.'
- Some remarkable Sandwiches were lately recorded

(by Dr J. Johnston) as having been made with satisfactory effect of cottonwool, for a patient who accidentally swallowed his false teeth through being struck in the face by a wave whilst swimming in the open sea. He was treated with Sandwiches containing a thin layer of cotton-wool in each, between the slices of bread and butter; and after a week, when a mild laxative was given, the dental structure, being now enrolled in cotton-wool, was passed without difficulty amongst the excrement.

• [From *Alice Through the Looking Glass*] . . . the White Knight had a little box 'of his own invention,' to keep clothes and Sandwiches in, 'You see,' he told Alice, 'I carry it upside down so that the rain can't get in.' 'But the things can get out,' Alice gently remarked; 'do you know the lid's open?'

However, it may be that Sheila Hutchins has the honour of recording an even greater oddity:

Probably none . . . was so strange as that sandwich well-known in the early 19th century and invented by a 'frail, fair one – the famous Mrs Sawbridge, we believe – who to show her contempt for an elderly adorer, placed the hundred pound note, which he had laid upon her dressing table, between two slices of bread and butter, and ate it as a sandwich.'

Sausages: These are normally fresh types for cooking; they differ from the general run of such sausages in having a significant cereal content. This difference has only been visible since the latter part of the 19th century, when industrial production of sausages began and manufacturers, anxious to have a mass market, sought to keep costs down. The idea of combining meat with cereal in a sausage-like casing was by no means a new one. Haggis is an antique and excellent example of the combination. But up to this time English sausages had been like Continental ones in being made more or less entirely of meat of some kind.

British pure pork sausages, similar to the French or Italian ones, are still made on a small scale, but the great majority of British sausages are made with rusk crumb or special 'sausage meal' (rather than the traditional breadcrumbs). The meat content of commercial sausages ranges from below 50% to 95% or more in the most expensive. Pork, or pork and beef, are considered best. Pure beef sausages are cheaper and are preferred in Scotland, where pork has been a less popular meat.

Traditional British sausages, all seasoned with pepper, usually black, and often with mace, include:

- Cambridge, with sage, cayenne, and nutmeg;
- Oxford, of pork, veal, and beef suet with sage, nutmeg, pepper, and sometimes herbs;
- Wiltshire, with ginger, and sometimes other seasonings;
- Yorkshire, with nutmeg, cloves, and cayenne;
- Lincolnshire, with sage and thyme;
- Manchester, with sage, cloves, nutmeg, and ginger;
- Cumberland, made of coarse-cut pork, and spicier

than most, not twisted into links, but sold by length from a long coil;

- Epping, an extinct but interesting variety, skinless, made of pork mixed with beef suet and bacon, with sage and spices;
- Glamorgan, a sausage containing cheese and leek (no meat or fish). This too is skinless, consolidated with a coating of egg white;
- tomato, a peculiar local variety which remains popular in the Midlands. It is a normal British pork sausage coloured reddish with tomato purée.

Shepherd's pie: a savoury dish of minced meat with a topping of mashed potato (now almost universal) or pastry (in Scotland in former times). In keeping with the name, the meat should be mutton or lamb; and it is usually cooked meat left over from a roast.

The name of the dish conjures up visions of shepherds of long ago eating this simple fare, but the name does not seem to have been used until the 1870s, when mincing machines were developed. The dish itself doubtless dates back much further, and it is generally agreed that it originated in the north of England and Scotland where there are large numbers of sheep. So the common idea that shepherds ate the dish back in, say, the 18th century is probably right.

The term cottage pie, often confused with shepherd's pie but properly denoting a similar dish made with minced beef, has a somewhat longer history and is similarly effective in evoking a rural and traditional context.

Shepherd's pie, well made from good ingredients, is delicious, easy, and inexpensive. But sometimes a dreadful travesty of it is served. Jane Grigson exhumed for her readers a report from the *Pall Mall Gazette* in 1885, to the effect that the Eastbourne Board of Guardians had ordered a mincing machine for the use of 'aged and toothless paupers' in their care. Commenting on this, she writes:

with the first mincing-machines, prison, school and seaside boarding house cooks acquired a new weapon to depress their victims, with water, mince, shepherd's pie with rubbery granules of left-over meat, rissoles capable of being fired from a gun.

The dish also crops up in Anglo-Indian cookery. Jennifer Brennan says that shepherd's pie was considered a great standby by Indian cooks and was often served for tiffin.

The equivalent dish in France is called *hachis Parmentier* in honour of the man who persuaded the French to eat potatoes.

Shrewsbury cakes: are a kind of biscuit (indeed occasionally known as Shrewsbury biscuits) of the shortbread type, made from flour, sugar, and butter, circular, fairly thin, and with scalloped edges. They are flavoured with spices, and sometimes rosewater. The earliest recorded recipe, given by Murrell (1621) uses nutmeg and rosewater.

A monograph on Shrewsbury cakes written by a Shrewsbury historian throws light on their early history. Since the 17th century Shrewsbury cakes always appear to have been known for their crisp, brittle texture, which is referred to by one Lord Herbet of Chirbury, who sent his guardian in 1602 'a kind of cake which our countrey people use and made in no place in England but in Shrewsbury . . . Measure not my love by substance of it, which is brittle, but by the form of it which is circular.'

By the end of the 17th century, the cakes were sufficiently well known for the playwright Congreve, in *The Way of the World*, to use the expression 'as short as a Shrewsbury cake', and for poets and musicians born in the W. Midlands to use them as motifs in their work. The recipe given by Eliza Smith calls for cinnamon as well as nutmeg.

A reference to the biscuits in the popular 19th-century series of poems *The Ingoldsby Legends* ensured their further fame. One of the poems therein mentions a maker of Shrewsbury cakes named Pailin; and a trade mark 'Pailin's Original Shrewsbury Cakes' was in use by the late 19th century.

Similar 'short cakes', of a crisp, friable texture, variously flavoured, were known in other parts of Britain.

Simnel cake: made for Easter, is a type of fruit cake similar to Christmas cake. It is distinguished by the use of marzipan or almond paste. Usually, half the raw cake mixture is put in the tin, covered with a sheet of marzipan, and the remaining mixture added. Towards the end of baking the top of the cake is covered with more marzipan, decorated with little marzipan balls, and browned lightly. Some omit the central layer of marzipan, and there is debate over the number of balls. Since they are said to represent the 12 apostles, some contend there should be 11 (thus excluding Judas); others say there should be 13 (to include Christ).

The marzipan is a late 19th-century embellishment of a food with a very long tradition, according to C. Anne Wilson. Medieval simnels appeared to be a type of light bread boiled and then baked. Spices and fruit probably become features of the recipes during the 17th century. From then on, there is evidence for several regional simnels, mostly using fruited, spiced yeast dough. Sometimes this was encased in a rich crust of pastry or dough similar to saffron bread, a form reminiscent of the Scottish black bun. The exception was on the island of Jersey, where the word 'simnel' meant a kind of biscuit until at least the mid-19th century.

Simnel cakes are particularly associated with the towns of Shrewsbury, which seems responsible for the cake as understood today; Devizes, which produced a star-shaped version without marzipan; and Bury, where a rubbed-in mixture, giving a result rather like a very rich scone, was baked in a long oval.

Originally simnel cakes belonged to Mothering Sunday (the fourth Sunday in Lent). Formerly marked by the population making pilgrimages to the mother church of their parishes, this became a day on which children working as servants and apprentices were given leave to visit their parents. Simnel cakes were taken as presents. Mothering Sunday has been eclipsed by the unrelated N. American custom of Mother's Day, and simnel cakes are now simply associated with Easter. There is, however, an isolated British survivor of a Mothering Sunday speciality, the 'mothering buns' made in the city of Bristol: these are rather plain yeast-leavened buns, iced, and sprinkled with hundreds and thousands, eaten for breakfast on that day.

Sin-eating: a curious practice by which a professional sin-eater was supposed to consume the sins of a person recently dead by consuming food before or at the funeral. Hone (1832) assembled evidence of this, largely pertaining to England but no doubt echoing similar customs elsewhere. His main English source, quoted both indirectly and directly, was John Aubrey (1626–97), from whom the two descriptions which follow derive.

Within the memory of our fathers, in Shropshire, in those villages adjoining to Wales, when a person died, there was notice given to an old 'sire' (for so they called him), who presently repaired to the place where the deceased lay, and stood before the door of the house, when some of the family came out and furnished him with a cricket (or stool), on which he sat down facing the door. Then they gave him a groat, which he put in his pocket; a crust of bread, which he ate; and a full bowl of ale, which he drank off at a draught. After this, he got up from the cricket, and pronounced, with a composed gesture, 'the ease and rest of the soul departed, for which he would pawn his own soul.'

In the county of Hereford was an old custom at funerals to hire poor people, who were to take upon them sins of the party deceased. One of them (he was a long, lean, ugly, lamentable poor rascal), I remember, lived in a cottage on Rosse highway. The manner was, that when the corpse was brought out of the house, and laid on the bier, a loaf of bread was brought out, and delivered to the sin-eater, over the corpse, as also a mazard bowl, of maple, full of beer (which he was to drink up), and sixpence in money: in consideration whereof he took upon him, ipso facto, all the sins of the defunct, and freed him or her from walking after they were dead.

There does not seem to be any record of what happened when a sin-eater, with his great accumulation of other people's sins, himself died. Perhaps the whole load was taken over by a younger member of the profession.

Sloe: or blackthorn, *Prunus spinosa*, a common wild hedgerow bush throughout Europe and W. Asia, is probably the only plum species native to Britain. Its small, black fruits are a byword for mouth-puckering astringency. Yet they make excellent jam, are infused to produce sloe gin, and are fermented to make other kinds of alcoholic drinks. Couplan writes that preserved in vinegar they are a good imitation of umeboshi.

Stargazey pie: a traditional British pie made with small, oily fish, whose heads are left poking up round the edge of the pie. Pilchards were the species originally used by the Cornish and Devon fisherfolk who invented the pie, but it was later made elsewhere with herring.

The standard explanation of this odd pie is that the heads of pilchards are uneatable, but full of rich oil which it would be a shame to waste. If the fish are arranged with their heads resting on the rim of a circular pie dish and projecting out of the crust (their tails clustered at the centre), the slope causes the oil to run down into the body of the fish; and when the pie is cut up the now useless heads can be discarded. However, experiments have shown that the amount of oil thus 'saved' is close to zero, which suggests that the only valid rationale for the pie is an aesthetic one.

The pie had a thin bottom crust and a thicker top one, both of shortcrust pastry. The fish were gutted and stuffed with a spoonful of herbs, or mustard, apple, or samphire.

The name 'stargazey' describes the star-shaped ring of fish heads peering out of the circumference of the pie, possibly gazing at the stars with the uppermost eye. In some versions the heads were grouped at the centre, dislocated to gaze upwards in a cluster, and the tails were set around the edge. The stargazey idea was also adapted into a straight form with the fish sandwiched between two strips of pastry, this could be divided into individual fish pasties and was suitable for sale from market stalls.

Steak and kidney pudding or pie: which counts as a British national dish, does not have a long history.

Beefsteak puddings (but without kidney) were known in the 18th century, if not before; Hannah Glasse gives a recipe, making clear that this was a suet pudding. A hundred years later, Eliza Acton gave a recipe for 'Ruth Pinch's Beefsteak Pudding', named for a character in Dickens's *Martin Chuzzlewit* and rather more extravagant than what she called 'Small Beef-Steak Pudding'. Neither had kidney. Shortly afterwards, however, Mrs Beeton did give a recipe for steak and kidney pudding, and this has kept a foothold in the British repertoire ever since. It was, however, overtaken in popularity by steak and kidney pie, which was easier to make. The filling for the pie is cooked separately, so that one can tell when the meat is tender, impossible in a sealed pudding. Only then is the meat put into a pie dish and the crust set over it. Then the pie is briefly baked to brown the pastry.

For both pudding and pie, the filling includes onion, and often mushrooms or oysters. Dorothy Hartley offers compelling advice on the choice and use of mushrooms and some words of warning about oysters (which may become too hard – indeed she suggests that it might be better to use cockles and rather implies that omitting any such molluscs would perhaps be better still). Besides this advice she provides one of her characteristic sets of drawings to show exactly how the pudding version would be organized.

The crust of the pie is usually made from flaky pastry, though other kinds are quite common. For a large pie, the top crust is attached to a band of pastry stuck around the inner rim of the dish, to keep the crust from shrinking off the rim.

Cockneys call steak and kidney pudding 'Kate and Sydney Pud'.

Stilton: an English cheese of international fame and the only British cheese to have legal protection, is officially described as follows:

Stilton is a blue or white cheese made from full-cream milk with no applied pressure, forming its own crust or coat and made in cylindrical form, the milk coming from English dairy herds in the district of Melton Mowbray and surrounding areas falling within the counties of Leicestershire (now including Rutland), Derbyshire and Nottinghamshire.

The Bell Inn, a coaching-house inn on the Great North Road, in the village of Stilton, seems to have become in the first quarter of the 18th century the main outlet for what was known locally as Quenby cheese. Quenby was 30 miles away, but as travellers became accustomed to buying the cheese at the Bell Inn it took on the name of Stilton. So much seems clear, but it is much more diffi-cult to unravel the actual origin of the cheese. Rance assembled the evidence and described the possibilities in a masterly way. He also provides the best account of the subsequent history of Stilton, of its manufacture, and of its characteristics.

Among the writers who took notice of Stilton at an

early stage was Daniel Defoe, who passed through Stilton in 1722 in the course of his *Tour through the Whole Island of Great Britain*, and Richard Bradley, who in the early 1720s was the first to publish a full recipe (which he claimed to have received from the Bell Inn) for making the cheese. It is interesting that he included mace in the recipe, and that the cheese continued to engage his attention, for in a later book he made some additions to the recipe.

Few farmhouses maintained the tradition of making Stilton in the rest of the 18th century and the 19th century, and there have not been many producers in the 20th century, although in the year 1980 total production amounted to 8,000 tons, which is a lot.

One occasionally reads about the practice of pouring some port wine into a Stilton through an aperture at the top. This is a foolish idea (which may have had its origin in a misplaced adaptation of an old custom – legitimate but no longer relevant – of letting wine drip on to the outside of the cheeses to assist crust formation). Mrs Beeton mentioned it, adding that sherry, Madeira, or old ale could also be used, but then seemed to drop the idea, asserting that 'that cheese is the finest which is ripened without any artificial aid'.

The use of a traditional silver scoop for lifting out servings of the cheese can be followed in restaurants or institutions where consumption is rapid. In domestic situations it is better to cut it across, removing a whole round for immediate consumption and then fitting the upper part back on to the lower part to ensure that what is left will keep well and not dry out.

White Stilton is an unblued cheese, with pleasant characteristics.

Suet puddings: a speciality of Britain, especially England, are traditionally based on beef suet. Its high melting point gives to suet puddings (and to suet crust and suet dumplings) a lightness not readily attainable with other fats. Among the oldest puddings in which suet was used were the ancient sausage-like white puddings. Suet paste appeared in the Middle Ages in small dumplings of the college pudding type; but it did not become really important until the introduction of the pudding-cloth at the beginning of the 17th century, which made large boiled puddings feasible.

Suet puddings (or dumplings – the terms are often interchangeable) might be absolutely plain, made only of suet and breadcrumbs and flour. Until the end of the 18th century, indeed until the early 20th century in some regions, it was customary in simple households to begin a meat meal with broth from the meat, followed by a plain suet pudding (boiled with the meat if appropriate), and only then, when appetite was largely satisfied by this filling combination, to serve the meat. Sheila Hutchins, in introducing an admirable chapter on suet puddings, has a fine quotation from Mrs Gaskell's *Cranford* embodying the slogan 'No broth, no [suet] ball; no ball no beef'. She describes how in farmhouse kitchens in Essex and Suffolk, her part of England, a suet pudding was usually boiled in a cloth in a long roly-poly shape and cut into slices a short while before the roasted meat was ready. The slices would be laid in the dripping-pan for a minute or two and browned. However, people who could not afford a joint for roasting could still have their dumplings:

Boiled currant dumpling or meat dumplings cooked in cotton bags in large copper pans used to be sold in the streets of London till about 1860 at a halfpenny each. Plum duff too, either round or roly poly shape, was popular in the London streets in the early nineteenth century and was sold together with a batter pudding made with raisins.

Well-known savoury suet puddings include steak and kidney pudding, bacon pudding and Suffolk onion pudding, to which Sheila Hutchins would add a good dozen more including partridge or pigeon puddings from the Ashdown Forest where special pudding basins used to be sold for making them; a formidable item called pork plugger; Shropshire herb roll; and Kentish rabbit pudding.

Turning to sweet suet puddings, the same author comments:

The heavy boiled sweet puddings thought to be typical of English cooking were rare in polite homes before the second quarter of the nineteenth century and reached the height of their popularity in the Victorian era, very probably under the influence of the rather Germanic court, on the arrival of the Prince Consort. Those in Victorian cookery books have a surprising number of German names – Kassel Pudding, Kaiser Pudding, Royal Coburg Pudding, Pudding à la Gotha, and of course Albert Pudding among others.

It is true that George I was known as Pudding George, but it can be maintained that the Hanover monarchy did not so much impose suet puddings on England as adopt what they thought to be a good thing when they arrived. The tradition goes back to the aforementioned (Oxford and Cambridge) college puddings, and of course includes the ancestors of Christmas pudding (which does include suet although this is very heavily outweighed by the other ingredients.

Efforts have for long been made, by one means or another, to prevent suet puddings becoming too soggy. Thus, Eliza Acton's 'The Welcome Guest's Own Pudding' of 1855 was enriched and lightened by the use of eggs and a complicated blend of fresh and dried crumbs and crushed ratafias.

Some English regional sweet suet puddings are baked, for example Tadcaster pudding, with mixed dried fruit and golden syrup, turned out after baking and covered with a spiced hot treacle sauce; and Cheltenham pudding, with fruit and crystallized ginger, served with brandy sauce.

The popularity of suet puddings and steamed puddings waned during the 20th century in Britain, but was having a well-deserved revival towards the end of the century.

Summer pudding: a favourite English dessert which combines a mixture of summer fruits with bread. Redcurrants and raspberries are the best fruits to use, but some varieties of gooseberry are suitable, and a small quantity of blackcurrants and a very few strawberries may be included. In autumn, blackberries can be substituted. In other countries, corresponding kinds of berry will do very well. In any case the fruit is lightly cooked with sugar.

The pudding is made by lining a buttered basin with fairly thin slices of good bread cut to fit exactly. The fruit and juice are then spooned in, and more bread placed over the top. The assemblage is then pressed down by a weight and left to stand overnight or longer. To serve, it is turned out, upside down. It is usually accompanied by cream.

In the 19th century this pudding seems to have been known as 'hydropathic pudding' because it was served at health resorts where pastry was forbidden. This name must have begun to seem unattractive or inappropriate early in the 20th century, when the new name summer pudding, which is now universally used, began to appear in print. Until recently it was thought that the earliest recorded use was by Florence Petty (1917) who, on the title page of her attractive book, styled herself 'The Pudding Lady' (and drew attention also to her qualifications as a Sanitary Inspector and a Horticulturist). However, it has now been established that a missionary in India, Miss E. S. Poynter (1904), had used the term much earlier, in her book; and that soon afterwards Miss L. Sykes (*c.*1912) used it as the title of a recipe which was even closer than Miss Poynter's to those now in use.

Sussex pond pudding: is so named because it has a large amount of butter in the middle which melts when the pudding is boiled, and soaks into the mixture. The original form of the pudding, as described in Ellis, was made from flour, milk, eggs, and a little butter, so that it was a predecessor of the 19th-century sponge pudding. More butter entered the mixture as the 'pond' melted. It was not sweetened, and was eaten either with meat or by itself.

Later, a sweetened suet pudding mixture lightened with baking powder became usual, and there was a further curious innovation. A thin-skinned lemon was placed, whole, in the centre of the 'pond'. It could be pricked all over so that the juice seeped out to flavour the mixture; but sometimes it was left unpierced, and exploded when boiled. This type of pudding was called 'lemon bomb'.

A variant made over the country border, Kentish well pudding, contains dried fruit instead.

Tennis cake: an English Victorian cake made to accompany the newly invented game of lawn tennis. Some authorities say that the original recipe is by Mrs Beeton herself, although it does not appear in the first edition of her book. It is a creamed cake made light by reserving the egg whites, and also raised with baking powder, containing finely chopped glacé cherries, sultanas and candied peel; it is flavoured with vanilla, cinnamon and maraschino or noyau liqueur, and topped with almond paste, glacé icing, glacé cherries and candied angelica. In the late 19th and early 20th centuries, tennis cakes, like other cakes and gateaux of the time, were very elaborate; one bakery textbook of the period gave 29 schemes for decorating the top of tennis cakes. By this time the cake had evolved from a round shape into an oblong approximating to the shape of a miniature tennis court.

Toad in the hole: a traditional British dish consisting of something in the way of meat (now usually sausages) baked in a batter pudding, provokes historical questions of exceptional interest. What are the origins of the dish and how did it get its name?

Enquiries are best commenced from two starting points. The first is that batter puddings (whether baked in the oven by themselves or cooked under the spit or jack in the drippings falling from a joint – in the latter case they could be classified as Yorkshire pudding) only began to be popular in the early part of the 18th century. Jennifer Stead has drawn attention to entries in *The Diary of Thomas Turner 1754–1765* and points out that Turner had sausages cooked in a baking tin with batter poured in and around them; not called toad in the hole by him but precisely foreshadowing what is now the most common form of that dish. Incidentally, Jennifer Stead's essay is the best reference for studying the complex historical questions surrounding batter pudding and Yorkshire pudding in Yorkshire.

The second is that the earliest recorded reference in print to toad in the hole occurs in a provincial glossary of 1787, quoted by the *OED* as saying: 'the dish called toad in a hole meat boiled in a crust.' That gives the

name, but the technique is different from that subsequently established. A slightly later citation in the *OED*,
recording what Mme. d'Arblay said in one of her letters,
about Mrs Siddons and the Sadler's Wells, has a batter
pudding (albeit of such enormous dimensions as to be
barely credible): 'as illfitted as the dish they called toad
in a hole . . . putting a noble sirloin of beef into a poor
paltry batter-pudding.'

Mrs Beeton describes the dish as 'homely but savoury'.
Her recipe had steak and kidney cooking in the batter,
but she said that leftover meat could be used.

Toast: as everyone in Britain knows, is made by placing
a slice of bread in front of dry heat – a fire, a grill, or an
electric toaster – until the surface browns and gives off
an attractive smell. The attractive taste, smell, and colour
of toast come from the thermal decomposition of sugar
and starch molecules on the surface of the bread.

The true toast addict is fussy about its preparation,
choosing day-old baker's bread to make it, and insisting
it is eaten as soon as ready, for good toast must be
consumed whilst hot. It is the smell of toast, and the
sensations of the hot crunchy outside of the bread combined with the soft inner crumb and melted butter, that
make it so appealing. Left to go cold, it becomes leathery
and loses its aroma.

Toast is a standard part of a proper English breakfast,
and together with a cup of tea, it forms a popular snack
at any time. Butter is the most common accompaniment;
other toppings include marmalade or jam or honey,

especially at breakfast time. Toast is often used, rather in the style of a medieval trencher, to provide an edible base for, say, poached eggs, sardines, baked beans, and other, mainly savoury, items.

Why toast should have become such an English speciality is not clear. Possibly English wheat bread, which kept for several days, had something to do with it. It certainly lends itself more to toasting than the close-textured rye breads, staple food in much of N. Europe. Elizabeth David says, 'I wonder if our open fires and coal ranges were not more responsible than the high incidence of stale bread for the popularity of toast in all classes of English household', and comments on the number of devices invented for holding bread in front of an open fire. These have now been replaced by the toaster, and the electric or gas grill.

Certainly, toast has a long history in Britain. 'Tost' was much used in the Middle Ages, being made in the ordinary way at an open fire. At this time sops – pieces of bread – were used to soak up liquid mixtures, and these were often first toasted, which reduced their tendency to disintegrate. Often toast was spread with toppings. 'Pokerounce' was toast with hot honey, spiced with ginger, cinnamon, and galingale. 'Toste rialle' was covered with a paste of sugar and rice flour moistened with sweet wine and including pieces of cooked quince, raisins, nuts, and spices, the whole thing covered with gilt sugar lozenges. A popular dish of the 17th century was cinnamon toast, which at that time was made by covering the toast with a paste of cinnamon and sugar moistened with wine. Early settlers in N. America retained their liking for it, and it became a traditional American dish.

Meat toppings for toast became fashionable during the 16th century. At first they were sweetened: for example veal toasts were made with chopped veal kidney and egg yolks, sugar, rosewater, cinnamon, and ginger. Various other 'hashes' based on finely chopped meat were served on toast. A trace of this practice survives in the serving of toast fingers with plain cooked minced meat, an adaptation made to the original dish in the 18th century.

The toast-and-something habit has a long precedent in England. Towards the end of the 16th century all kinds of things began to appear on toast, such as poached eggs (which had been previously served in broth); buttered (scrambled) eggs; ham or bacon; anchovies; and melted cheese. All of them have remained associated with toast. The last achieved existence as a separate dish known as Welsh rabbit (or rarebit) which it has maintained until this day. Toast with toppings became very popular as 'savoury toast', beloved of the Victorians and Edwardians. This, remarked 'Wyvern':

belongs wholly to English cookery . . . savoury toasts of an ordinary kind ought to be favourably regarded by all thrifty housekeepers, inasmuch as they afford an easy and pleasant way of working up fragments of good food that might otherwise be wasted.

Throughout the Middle Ages and early modern period, toast was often moistened in wine when making such dishes as toasted cheese, but at the end of the 17th century it became more usual to butter it. Hot buttered toast was eaten at breakfast. Later, when afternoon tea became the fashion, it appeared here too.

The 1890s saw the arrival of Melba toast. This is extraordinarily thin toast and a technique for producing it is often attributed to Escoffier and Ritz, who are supposed to have named it for Marie Ritz (who had been demanding thinner toast) but then renamed it for Melba at a time when her diet called for something of the sort. Elizabeth David found the story appealing but questionable.

Toast also has a slightly disreputable history as a basis for drinks. Amongst many coffee substitutes used in the 18th century, burnt toast soaked in water was the easiest to make. The result was not much like coffee; but then neither were any of the other drinks made from grains, roots, and herbs. However, towards the end of the century toast water (see below) was made as a drink in its own right.

Toast water: an example of a whole category of supposedly health-restoring foods. Water in which cereals have been cooked or soaked plays a leading role in traditional folk medicine in many countries, and with good reason. Illness drains the body's energy and fluids. To counter this, water prevents dehydration and starch helps to restore strength. In the past, if you wished someone well, it seemed natural to drink his or her health in a liquid in which bread, the staple food, had been steeped;

toasting and flavouring the bread, and substituting wine for water, made the wish more effective and the drink more palatable. We therefore still toast our friends on formal occasions. Rice water is still given to invalids in many parts of Asia and Africa. Barley water (usually flavoured and fortified with lemon – for vitamin C – and sugar) was a popular energy-giving drink in Britain until about 1980.

Toast water was made in most bread-eating households throughout the 18th and most of the 19th centuries. Boiling water was poured onto toasted bread and allowed to cool. It was then strained, and was ready to drink, though flavourings were often added – sugar and cream, lemon, dried orange peel, currant jelly, or roasted apples. Alexis Soyer (1849) gave precise instructions for making it, and insisted the toast must not be burnt, stating that:

the idea that bread must be burnt black to make toast water is quite a popular delusion, for nothing nourishing could come from it: if your house was burnt to ashes, it would be valueless; and the same with burnt bread, which merely makes the water black, but the nutriment of the bread, intended to relieve the chest, has evaporated in smoke by being burnt.

However, Dr and Mrs Delamere (1878) contradicted this, alleging that bread charcoal is an efficient water purifier, and that the toast should actually be set on fire. This issue is amusingly described by Helen Pollard (1993) in a well-researched exegesis in which she comments:

In support of Soyer and other writers, it is true that the brown colour of toast is partly due to the conversion of insoluble starch into soluble dextrins which would contribute a (negligible) amount to the nutritive value of the preparation. The main benefit from drinking toast water would, however, be the replacement of body fluids. The final word on toast water must belong to the Delameres. 'If the toast-and-water is required to appear in decanters, as "President's sherry", it should be poured away from the bread as soon as it has sufficient colour.'

The notion of toast water lingered into the late 20th century in a number of patent health foods, but the decline of protracted minor illnesses and the use of antibiotics have made these liquid diets less necessary.

Toffee apple: a popular confection in Britain, especially in the autumn, when they used to be prominent, with their vivid red colour, at autumn fairs. A whole fresh apple, on a thin stick, is dipped in high-boiled sugar syrup which has been coloured red; and allowed to set before being wrapped in cellophane.

The *OED* gives no quotations relating to toffee apples earlier than the beginning of the 20th century. However, the use of the term as soldier's slang for a type of bomb used in the First World War suggests that they were already well known, and probably have a longer history than the quotations allow.

In the phrase 'toffee apple' the word 'toffee' means simple boiled sugar, not the mixture of sugar and dairy produce which is what the word usually refers to. This may be another indication of an older origin of the toffee apple.

There is some similarity between toffee apples and the Chinese dessert items which consist of pieces of banana or apple fried in batter and then coated in caramelized syrup. Whether there is any historical connection is not clear.

Twelfth Night cake: a cake made for Twelfth Night, the last of the twelve days of Christmas. Now a celebration of Epiphany, the occasion when the three Kings visited the infant Jesus, this festival has inherited some of the pagan customs associated with Roman Saturnalia, when slaves were allowed many privileges including eating with and gambling against their masters. Dice were thrown to choose a 'king', and everyone had to obey his command. The two ancient traditions involving kings were interwoven to give the modern Twelfth Night custom of choosing a 'king' by dividing a cake containing a token – a dried bean or a china doll. The finder gains privileges or pays forfeits, depending on the custom of the country. Sometimes a dried pea, for a queen, is also included.

The custom of the 'Twelfth cake', complete with bean, flourished for centuries in England. During the late 17th century, the series of tokens included in the cake (at this time, a fruit cake leavened with yeast) expanded. Henry Teonge, a naval chaplain, wrote in 1676 that we had a great cake made, in which was put a bean for the King, a pea for the queen, a clove for a knave, a forked stick for the cuckold and a rag for the slut. The cake was cut into several pieces in the great cabin, and all put into a napkin, out of which each took his piece, as out of a lottery; then each piece is broken to see what was in it, which caused much laughter, to see our Lieutenant prove the cuckold, and more to see us tumble one over the other in the cabin, by reason of the rough weather.

During the 18th century the tokens became a series of characters printed on paper which were cut out, folded, and drawn from a hat. The custom eventually declined in the middle of the century, though a vestige survives in the coins or tokens that are still put into a Christmas pudding. In 1794 the actor Robert Baddeley left £100 to be invested to provide a cake for all those acting at Drury Lane Theatre on Twelfth Night.

Worcester(shire) sauce: originated in the 1840s. The story goes that it was the result of an accidental oversight in a Worcester chemist's shop, Lea Perrin's. A barrel of spice vinegar, made according to an Indian recipe for a customer but never collected, was left for some years in the cellar. It began to ferment; possibly, some say, because one of the ingredients was soy sauce. The shopkeeper was about to throw out the spoiled barrel, but fortunately tasted the contents and discovered that they had undergone an intriguing change. He therefore bottled them, sold them as a sauce, and began to produce more.

Worcester sauce is now widely used not only in English cooking but all over the world, sometimes in locally manufactured versions. In Japan, for instance, soy sauce and Worcester sauce (known to the Japanese as *ustasosu*) are the two standard sauces to be found on dining tables; Hosking gives historical background for the latter and explains its particular appeal to the Japanese palate on the ground that it enhances the flavour known to the Japanese as *umami*. Yan-Kit So describes the corresponding phenomenon in China:

In many Cantonese kitchens Lea & Perrins Worcestershire sauce stands as a twin to the soy sauce bottle, and is used most popularly as a dipping sauce for deep-fried food such as spring rolls and prawn balls.

Being highly concentrated, Worcester sauce is employed mostly as a condiment or an ingredient rather than as a relish like the brown sauce which it superficially resembles.

The ingredients are supposedly secret, and it is said that no imitations of the original brand have achieved quite the same flavour.

Yorkshire Christmas pie: a huge raised pie in the medieval tradition, which outlasted other kinds and became so popular in Yorkshire in the 18th century that pies were sent to London as festive Christmas fare. It was still being made in the closing years of the 19th century. It was one of those feats of 'Russian doll' stuffing which are better known as being made for Arab wedding feasts. A typical recipe is in Hannah Glasse's *The Art of Cookery*. A very thick crust enclosed a turkey, which was stuffed with a goose, the goose with a fowl, then a partridge, then a pigeon. All these birds were boned. On one side of the turkey was a hare cut in pieces; on the other woodcocks, moorhens, or other small wild game. At least 2 kg (4 lb) of butter were also put in before the massive lid was closed and the pie baked. Not all pies were made with boned birds, so that some pies had to be dismantled and the various creatures removed to carve them, detracting from the pie's appeal.

Yorkshire pudding: is made from an egg, flour, and milk batter cooked in a large shallow tin containing a layer of very hot beef dripping. It is a popular accompaniment to roast beef in Britain, and the two together compose the 'traditional' Sunday lunch. Sometimes the batter is poured into smaller, round tins to make individual puddings but this is not the authentic Yorkshire method. Strictly speaking, the pudding, cut in squares, should be served with gravy before the meat, to take the edge off the appetite.

Batter puddings have a long history and exist in many forms, mostly sweet. According to C. Anne Wilson it would have been cooks in the north of England who devised the form for which Yorkshire became famous. She draws attention to a recipe for 'A Dripping Pudding' which was published in *The Whole Duty of a Woman*:

Make a good batter as for pancakes; put it in a hot toss-pan over the fire with a bit of butter to fry the bottom a little, then put the pan and butter under a shoulder of mutton, instead of a dripping pan, keeping frequently shaking it by the handle and it will be light and savoury, and fit to take up when your mutton is enough; then turn it in a dish and serve it.

At this time, meat was roasted on a spit, or by suspending it from a jack in front of the fire, so the instruction to place the pudding under the meat meant that it was some inches below, not poured around the joint in the same baking tin. Hannah Glasse gave a similar recipe, calling it A Yorkshire pudding'. She makes it clear that it should be brown and dry, and remarks that: 'It is an exceeding good pudding, the gravy of the meat eats well with it.'

Jennifer Stead discusses the origin and development of the dish. Commenting on the localized attribution of 'Yorkshire' attached to it, she notes that batter puddings were also known in the south of England; Yorkshire batter puddings appear to have been distinguished by their lightness and crispness. This is obtained by introducing the batter into a pan containing fat which is smoking hot, thus starting to form a crust underneath straight away; as the pudding continues to cook, the air incorporated into the batter during mixing expands, making it rise, and the fierce heat dries out the top of the pudding leaving it crunchy. Stead relates the technique to the people:

This accords with their fabled brusque temperaments: the fact that they require spanking hot fat, explosions as the batter hits it, fierce heat, and crisp results, may explain why it has often been said that only Yorkshire folk – those possessing the Yorkshire temperament – can make a true Yorkshire pudding.

Such details had not escaped Hannah Glasse, who herself came from the north of England and who said that the dripping must boil before the batter is added.

Yorkshire people frequently castigate southerners for not being able to make proper Yorkshire puddings. Stead suggests that one reason for this is that cooks in the south are accustomed to making perfectly legitimate batter puddings of softer texture, which were never intended to be crisp and well risen. She thinks, however, that the main reason may be that throughout the 19th century cookery writers (mostly from the south) mis-understood and distorted the recipes for true Yorkshire pudding. As she says: it is clear that some writers had never clapped eyes on, let alone cooked, a Yorkshire pudding.'

New kitchen technology in the shape of the enclosed coal range, and later the gas or electric oven, changed the Yorkshire pudding in one essential. It was no longer possible to cook it under the roasting meat, and therefore it no longer received the juice dripping from the joint.

Yorkshire pudding was never eaten exclusively with beef. The early recipe for batter pudding mentions mutton; indeed, it could be served before any roast meat, in which case an appropriate sauce (mint, for lamb, or apple, for pork) might be served with it. Sugar, vinegar, jam, mustard, or golden syrup were other options, although the pudding was always eaten before the meat in Yorkshire, whatever was eaten with it.

For a Yorkshire pudding mixture with sausages embedded in it, see toad in the hole; this is but one of scores of variations on an outstandingly popular theme.

THE STORY OF PENGUIN CLASSICS

Before 1946 …'Classics' are mainly the domain of academics and students, without readable editions for everyone else. This all changes when a little-known classicist, E. V. Rieu, presents Penguin founder Allen Lane with the translation of Homer's *Odyssey* that he has been working on and reading to his wife Nelly in his spare time.

1946 The *Odyssey* becomes the first Penguin Classic published, and promptly sells three million copies. Suddenly, classic books are no longer for the privileged few.

1950s Rieu, now series editor, turns to professional writers for the best modern, readable translations, including Dorothy L. Sayers's *Inferno* and Robert Graves's *The Twelve Caesars*, which revives the salacious original.

1960s 1961 sees the arrival of the Penguin Modern Classics, showcasing the best twentieth-century writers from around the world. Rieu retires in 1964, hailing the Penguin Classics list as 'the greatest educative force of the 20th century'.

1970s A new generation of translators arrives to swell the Penguin Classics ranks, and the list grows to encompass more philosophy, religion, science, history and politics.

1980s The Penguin American Library joins the Classics stable, with titles such as *The Last of the Mohicans* safeguarded. Penguin Classics now offers the most comprehensive library of world literature available.

1990s Penguin Popular Classics are launched, offering readers budget editions of the greatest works of literature. Penguin Audiobooks brings the classics to a listening audience for the first time, and in 1999 the launch of the Penguin Classics website takes them online to an ever larger global readership.

The 21st Century Penguin Classics are rejacketed for the first time in nearly twenty years. This world famous series now consists of more than 1,300 titles, making the widest range of the best books ever written available to millions – and constantly redefining the meaning of what makes a 'classic'.

The Odyssey continues …

The best books ever written

PENGUIN (🐧) CLASSICS

SINCE 1946